Tribute:
Three Lives Remembered

Tribute: Three Lives Remembered

A STORY OF POVERTY, PASSION, AND HOPE

JUDYTHE PEARSON PATBERG

Tribute: Three Lives Remembered

Copyright © 2019 by Judythe Pearson Patberg.
All rights reserved.

To order copies of additional books by the author - We Just Shoveled Two Feet of Partly Cloudy, From Peace Corps with Love, A Winter Sabbatical, Rushing to Sunset, and The Years Come and Go - please contact: (Mostly) Minnesota Editions; 261 Stags Run; Harbor Springs, MI; 49740; Judythe.patberg@gmail.com

No part of this publication may be reproduced, stored in a retrieval system or transmitted in any way by any means, electronic, mechanical, photocopy, recording or otherwise without the prior permission of the author except as provided by USA copyright law.

The opinions expressed by the author are not necessarily those of URLink Print and Media.

1603 Capitol Ave., Suite 310 Cheyenne, Wyoming USA 82001
1-888-980-6523 | admin@urlinkpublishing.com

URLink Print and Media is committed to excellence in the publishing industry.

Book design copyright © 2019 by URLink Print and Media. All rights reserved.

Published in the United States of America

ISBN 978-1-64367-662-3 (Paperback)
ISBN 978-1-64367-663-0 (Digital)

01.08.19

The past is always with us never to be escaped; it alone is enduring; but, amidst the changes and chances which succeed one another so rapidly in this life, we are apt to live too much for the present and too much in the future. On such an occasion as the present.... it is good to hark back to the olden days and to gratefully recall the men whose labours in the past have made the present possible.

> Dr. William Osler, 1889.1

War, in its most atrocious form, again hovers over the earth like a devastating demon of destruction.

> Florence Lind, *circa* 1968

To the memories of Ernie Pearson and all the boys of the 30s who died from lack of medical knowledge or the impact of poverty brought about by the Great Depression…. to the memory of Raymond Pearson, a part of whose story I'm proud to tell, and to all those who served our country in some capacity during World War II.

Ernie Pearson
1932
Minneapolis

Raymond Pearson
1974
On His Farm

Introduction

In early May, 1932, a fifteen-year-old boy left his small farm in northern Minnesota for a large hospital in Minneapolis. He had been diagnosed with Hodgkin lymphoma (also known as Hodgkin's lymphoma and previously known as Hodgkin's disease) and was undergoing radiation treatments that produced pain and uncertainty. Even more acutely felt than the pain and uncertainty, however, was the mind-wrenching homesickness. Through it all, Ernie sustained the hope that he would get well, so that he could return to his beloved farm where the people he loved most in this world were waiting for him.

At the same time, another fifteen-year-old boy was fighting for his life in a hospital room not far from Ernie's. Though different as night and day, the two boys shared a nostalgia for the home they were forced to leave, each for a different reason. Tom was an irrepressible storyteller, whose stories fascinated Ernie because they spoke of a life with which he was totally unfamiliar. He felt sorry for Tom who had a family that didn't seem to care. In Ernie's mind, this reality was as baffling as Tom's stories were fascinating. Thirteen years later, in 1945, a second transplant occurred. This time it was Ernie's brother, Raymond (Fat), who left the small farm in northern Minnesota to serve in World War II. Fat's letters are replete with references to a brother with whom he shared a childhood that could best be characterized as a time of innocence and play.

In telling my story, I have relied upon information contained in letters sent home by Ernie Pearson in 1932 and by Raymond Pearson in 1945-46. Nothing in the letter excerpts has been substantially changed. I have also relied on personal knowledge of these two individuals obtained through interviews and conversations with my father, Ernie's and Raymond's brother, and with my Uncle Raymond who just recently died. Ernie was an uncle I never knew; Raymond was one that I knew well. All of the descriptions of the farm are accurate, having grown up in that place and knowing first-hand the people who lived there.

The character of Tom is revealed through Ernie's letters, and that is the only information we have about his personal life, including no mention of a last name. In order to more fully develop Tom's character, I have used background material from several books about the Great Depression and teenagers who rode trains in search of food during that bleak time in our history. The books that helped me most to understand the 1930s Depression Era were *Riding the Rails* by Errol Lincoln Uys, *Children of the Great Depression* by Russell Freedman, *The Worst Hard Time* by Timothy Egan, and *A Hobo Memoir 1936* by John Fawcett. I read parts of these books several times in order to immerse myself in a portrait of hardship, courage, and hope during one of our nation's bleakest times. My personal contact with Don Snyder, who rode the rails as a teenager, took place in an interview at his home in Toledo, Ohio.

I also read a number of books about World War II which gave me background information to expand upon, clarify, and illustrate the contents of Raymond's letters. Three that were particularly helpful were *Chronicles of War*, edited by Duncan Hill, *War and Remembrance* by Herman Wouk, and *The Greatest Generation* trilogy by Tom Brokaw.

A final source of information for depicting the lives of people who were important to Ernie and Raymond is a family memoir I co-authored and edited several years ago, *We Just Shoveled Two Feet of Partly Cloudy: A (Mostly) Minnesota Memoir.*

All of the above-mentioned works, as well as others, are referenced in the Reference section at the end of the book. When I credited the parts of my text that I wrote on the basis of having read these works, I noted the source that was most responsible for my summary of information. These sources are cited in the Notes section at the end of the book.

My attempt has been to portray, through primary and secondary sources as well as personal relationships, the lives of two teenage boys brought together under tragic circumstances during the summer of 1932. One of these boys had a special bond with a brother who, thirteen years later, reflected upon this bond in letters he sent home while serving in World War 11. The memories of Ernie and Raymond Pearson will live on in their letters and in the hearts and minds of those who loved them. Tom's memory is more elusive. I think it would be amazing if someone reading this book would recognize Tom as family or a friend, thereby giving him a last name and his own identity. Perhaps that person would feel happy to have a missing piece of Tom's life filled in and recorded. If that doesn't happen, then Tom will be remembered as one of the 250,000 brave boys who rode the rails during the Great Depression. Either way, his memory will also live on.

Judythe Pearson Patberg
April 24, 2013

Part One

Ernie and Tom

In the late 1800s, Sven and Hedvig Pearson emigrated from Sweden and Norway, respectively, and settled in Fargo, North Dakota, where Sven worked as an iceman. Motivated by a restlessness and desire for a better life, they moved to Minneapolis, where they lived for a short time before taking advantage of the Homestead Act, which promised them free land in northern Minnesota if they would clear it, build a home, and live on it for at least five years. The year was 1913, and Sven and Hedvig set up roots in the Bemis Hill area of northern Minnesota but didn't homestead very long because the conditions turned out to be unsuitable for farming. So back to Minneapolis they went.

Sven's job as a park caretaker in Minneapolis provided a lovely home for his family, which included five boys: Edwin, Oscar, Ernest, Raymond, and Roy. As the years went by, however, the older boys became increasingly involved with unsavory characters in the city, and Sven and Hedvig worried that they were turning into "hoodlums." Whether it was this worry over their sons' reputations or Sven's seemingly peripatetic nature—or a combination of both factors—a move was once again in the picture for the Pearsons. Their home this time was 160 acres they were able to purchase in Falun Township, back in northern Minnesota. It was the last move that Sven and Hedvig would make.

Sven and Hedvig, along with their five boys, left Minneapolis for Falun in the spring of 1930. Raymond tells the story of their trip in the book, *We Just Shoveled Two Feet of Partly Cloudy:*[2]

Someone told Pa that if he would buy a plow and a harrow to prove that his intentions to be a farmer were sincere, he could rent a whole boxcar for 25 dollars. He did just that, and, after asking for God's help on the trip, we left Minneapolis in a 1926 Model T Ford with no top and no side curtains, the absence of which wasn't a problem since it was spring and the weather was warm. We made it to Badger, about 30 miles from home, on the same day, but with no headlights we couldn't continue and had to stay overnight. The next morning we arrived at our destination in Falun Township. A few days later the boxcar with our furniture and plow and harrow arrived in Roseau, and we hauled everything home with a team of horses and a wagon that Pa had recently purchased.

Hilding Ernest Pearson (Ernie), born on July 13, 1916, was thirteen when they arrived at their new home. He had two years to enjoy the farm and hunting with his brothers, especially Raymond, before he was diagnosed with Hodgkin lymphoma. Hedvig took him to the hospital at the University of Minnesota in Minneapolis on the train and stayed with him for two weeks. Ernie underwent treatments at the hospital, and between treatments he often stayed with his Uncle John (Sven's brother) and Aunt Carrie. He was only 300 miles from home, but he might as well been clear across the country because no one—neither his parents nor his brothers—had the money or the wherewithal to visit him during his three-month absence. So he wrote sentimental letters, using a simple folksy style of writing—letters that were flooded with a sense of nostalgia. He wrote from the heart for those he loved and for himself, evoking childhood memories and conveying hope.... always conveying hope.

May 19, 1932
Dear Pop and Brothers:

How is it that you don't write to me? I sure have been waiting. Mom got Pop's letter and she told me all about it. Poor Hovda! It's too bad but it couldn't be helped.

Mom told me that all the turkey hens are sitting and I sure am glad about that. I feel much better now than I did when I was home. And Boy, what an appetite! I can eat anything that's set before me. I'm in the hospital now and am getting along well. There's eight of us in a big room and we live good. And talk about good nurses, they are always nice. You were right when you bragged about the University, Pop. It sure is some hospital.

Well, how is everything getting along? Is Roy still trapping gophers? I suppose he is tramping the Grade now. Us brothers may fight and quarrel but I'm sure we love each other, down in the bottom of our hearts, especially me and you, Fat. A pastor came in and talked with me today. It was the first one I seen in the hospital. I suppose there's lots of them though.

Has Ocky dropped a "slasher" yet? I bet there's lots of them down there now. I reckon they've all come from the ridge now. I can just picture "Sir Potley" with his nose down in the grass and two barrels sticking way out on each side. Mom borrowed $10 from Nels and Mae about a week ago. They sure are nice people. You should see how fat Aunty Carrie is now! She's been drinking eggnog for over eight months and she's as fat as she can be. I think I'll start in with that too. If you guys want to faint take a squint at Elmer Pearson. He's about as tall as you guys and he weighs 190 pounds. He's so big and fat he can hardly stand. But he sure has changed, he's a dandy kid now. He aint stuck up no more.

Maybe you're wondering why this is such poor writing? Well, I'll tell you. It's because I am laying in bed when I am writing. Therefore I can't keep steady. I sure hope everything turns out good with the turkeys so's to bring a little money. How is my little calf? I suppose he is growing a little.

I feel sure that God is going to let me come home to the farm again and see my Pop and brothers. I know this is a punk letter but read it anyway. "AND PLEASE

WRITE TO ME" because I sure like to hear from any of you. It is a relief to get a letter once in a while. I will close with much love to all, from Ernie.

(Note: Slasher-Ernie's name for deer; Sir Potley-Ernie's pig; Aunty Carrie is pregnant; Elmer Pearson-cousin; Hovda-Sam Hovda, Vivian Pearson's father)

There was a lot to do for a thirteen-year-old boy when the Pearson family moved from Minneapolis to the farm in the spring of 1930. Sven and the older boys cleared the land for building and farming. Ernie and Raymond helped Hedvig with the chores, but mostly they hunted and talked about hunting. They were as different as night and day. Raymond writes in *Partly Cloudy:* "I was robust with a hearty appetite, while he was thin and always pale." He said that Hedvig used to worry about Ernie's lack of appetite, and Ernie didn't do much to relieve her fears when he reminded her that she shouldn't expect him to eat every day.

Ernie had felt tired during the winter of 1932 and often woke up at night covered in sweat. He experienced occasional back pain and abdominal discomfort—symptoms of early stage Hodgkin. Then one day he noticed a swollen area on the side of his neck and told Sven who immediately took him in to Roseau to see Dr. Berge. It was at the doctor's office that Ernie admitted he often had no appetite, even for Hedvig's homemade bread and potato soup. He had lost weight, as evidenced by the clothing which hung so loosely on his thin frame. Dr. Berge suspected Hodgkin lymphoma, and his diagnosis was confirmed by a biopsy at the University of Minnesota.

Laughing at the memory of hunting stories years later, Raymond said that Ernie's lack of desire for food didn't take away any of his passion for hunting. He recalls the time he and Ernie went hunting without packing a lunch, as they usually did. They hunted all day and Raymond's stomach was growling with hunger. All he could think about were the dumplings that he knew Hedvig was making for supper. When he suggested to Ernie that they go home before their brothers and whoever else was staying at the house ate all of the dumplings, Ernie scoffed and accused Fat of thinking only of food. He convinced Fat that they should make two more drives before they headed for home. Weak with hunger and sick with the fear that all sustenance would be gone by the time they reached home, Fat barely made it into the house, where Hedvig put before him a plate of dumplings that she had saved for him and Ernie. Raymond remembers that Ernie ate only one or two, while he shoveled the rest. His voice was wistful. "I wish that I could have given Ernie some of my love for food," he said. But, of course, he couldn't have.

Ernie must have known that his family worried about his lack of appetite and saw that as an indication of his illness. In an attempt to ease their worry in his letters, he continually tried to reassure them that his appetite was increasing, which meant that he was getting well. Sometimes his attempts to impress them with his newfound appetite were humorous. In one letter, for example, he says: *To tell you guys the truth I am getting scared of my own appetite. I betcha I eat enough for two of you, Fat. I'll tell you what I ate for supper. 1. Two heaping plates of noodles with hamburgers in them. 2. Six slices of bread. 3. One heaping plate of potatoes and meat. 6. One plate of rhubarb and sauce. 7. And one bowl of tomato soup. That aint so bad, is it? Even for you, Fat, that's a lot of food so you know I'm getting better.*

He makes a point of exaggerating his food intake several times in his letters, while generally downplaying his illness, in a desperate attempt to convince his family that he was getting well. He also tried to share with his family as much information about his disease and treatment as he was able to provide, given his limited vocabulary and knowledge, thinking that the more they knew, the more reassured they would be that his stay in the hospital would be short-lived and curative.

May 27, 1932
Dear Pop and Brothers:

I know a little more today because of an ex-ray picture. They took a picture of my chest. Here is the main point: The doctors have to have a piece of that tumor that Dr. Berge extracted. It may be four sicknesses and it may be one the doctors say. They have to find out exactly which one it is and when they do they will apply treatments and by the way they talk it seems as though I'll recover, and in the meantime I may be up and around the doctor says. My sickness is nothing compared with some that come in the University. I met three different persons today that had tumors in the throat. They could hardly breathe. A man had gallstones so bad that it inflamed his whole chest. The doctors operated on him, and they froze it so perfect that he didn't even know when they began. He laid there until they were through and he didn't feel one pain. He is going home in a few days. People come in here half dead with every kind of sickness on earth and they come out cured. Of course it all depends on God. A man in the ward has got "T.B. of the bones." He has been on his back in bed for 4 years without moving. If he moves all is lost. If it is not checked in time the T.B. melts the joints together in one stiff mass. So after a while he is just like a board. One guy I met has a sickness I'm not sure about. He's about my age and his name is Tom. Sure is friendly, wants to talk all the time, mostly about Chicago where he's from. This hospital is wonderful.

We was down to Frank Kings the other day but Frank wasn't home so we talked with Mrs. King. Frank pretty near had T.B. this winter, he kept going to the University. Mrs. King pretty near died of "gall stone" and cancer of the liver this winter. She had four hard spells. A guy sure has to have patience in the University but it's a good thing because this is the best place to be sick. The doctors that are smarter than the others are always called in to examine the patient.

I will close this time with love to all. From Ernie.

(Note: The Kings were Hedvig's friends whom she befriended while staying with Ernie in Minneapolis for two weeks.)

From his room at the University of Minnesota Hospital, Ernie could look across the Mississippi River and see Fairview, which at that time was the teaching hospital of the U of M Medical School. In 1979, the Hospital and Fairview merged to form the University of Minnesota Medical Center, Fairview. It is one of the most respected teaching institutions in the nation. Its focus is, and has always been, on balancing responsiveness to patients' needs with access to state-of-the-art treatments and technology in order to provide the best care and results. Ernie possessed a great deal of faith in his doctors, always reassuring his parents that they were the best, and it turns out that his faith was not misplaced: They *were* the best that the field of medicine could offer in 1932.

(Note: This information was obtained through several phone calls to the University of Minnesota Medical School in an unsuccessful attempt to access Ernie's medical records.)

With all of the time that Ernie had to lie in his bed and think—did he wonder about such things as how he would feel during therapy and how he would know if the treatments were working? Did he question what the treatment would actually do for him? Did he worry about the risks and possible side effects?

May 30, 1932
Dear Pop and Brothers:

I am getting along fine and I hope you are also. I received your letter, Ed and it did me good to read it. I am getting along fine in the hospital. I mostly walk around the halls in a pair of pajamas and a robe doing nothing. The nurses sometimes bring in some very light work to do and I while away the time that way. The treatments I am taking are fine and I sure am improving. I never have any backaches or anything like that. I sleep like a log and eat like a bear. You know that gland I have? Well, it's about half size now. I have had three treatments already and I didn't feel one of them. I go alone to the treatment place now because it's just down at the end of the hall. I get on a elevating bed which can be moved up or down. Next I am stripped from the waist down and a huge black tank is moved directly over me. Then the doctor shuts all doors in the room and locks everything. He then goes to a small control room and turns on the electricity, inside of the tank can be heard a queer noise, which sounds exactly like a wash machine. Under the tank is a little round light and from that light issues the treatment I am to have. It is run by electric currents. Inside of that tank is a big bulb with currents of electricity. He leaves it on for fifteen minutes then you are allowed to go. The only thing that you feel after the treatment is that the place where it was turned on is quite hot. That very night after the treatment I could feel that the gland went down and I sure am glad because I believe that it is God's will that I should return to the farm.

Mom told me that she has to return to you again because of Rolla and the turkeys. I am glad that Mom is going because it depends on her if the turkeys are going to get along good or not. And in another way I feel bad about it because I sure would like to have her stay. How is everything on the farm? Boy! I wish I was there. I like the farm ten times more than the city. Is the weather nice up there? I suppose it is by now. I hope I can come home again and I think I will. There's a man in our ward that reminds me of you, Pop. Every time I look at him I think of you because of his mustache which looks just like yours. And he resembles you in appearance. Is Ock still courting Vivian? Hang on, Ock and you'll have her.

Do you remember that I told you about Tom? That guy sure is interesting. He came to our ward and talked until the nurses came to get him. He sure is a talker likes to talk about Chicago where he's from. His dad was a fireman who lost his job and Tom had to leave home because there wasn't enough food for him and all his brothers and sisters. His mom fixed hair but now there wasn't enough women who go have their hair done. I feel sorry for him. He went to California to find jobs but there aint any jobs there anymore so he came back. Now here's the part that will make you faint. He rides trains but don't pay. He passed out when he was waiting for a train in Minneapolis, so the engineer took him here to the hospital. He's been here for a month and is pretty homesick for his mother. He sent some money home when he had some to spare but it hasn't been much.

I suppose Fat's using my rifle. But that's all right. But be sure you clean it well and don't clean it from the front. A librarian comes around with a mass of books and I pick out four each time. But I have something else and that's the Sunday School papers that the pastor brings around. Be good to yourselves, Pop and brothers and I am sure we will meet again. Well, I must close this time. With much love to you all. Write when you have time. From Ernie.

If Ernie had gotten sick today, he would have had an 80% to 90% chance of being cured. In 1932, however, he had no chance, outside of a miracle. "If Ernie has what I think he has," said Dr. Berge when Sven brought him in for an examination, "he has a one in a million chance of being cured." It turned out that Ernie did have what Dr. Berge thought he had: Hodgkin lymphoma. Raymond recalled the moment his mother told him and his brothers the news about Ernie's diagnosis. "I remember believing that Ernie would survive because he was a fighter and tough as nails. And then, there was always God. If the doctors couldn't help Ernie, God could. So we were all hopeful."

Hodgkin lymphoma is a rare cancer affecting the lymph system in the body. It is most common among young adults (15-35) and men over 50. It is characterized by the painless enlargement of lymph nodes, occurring most often above the collar bone and sometimes, in younger patients such as Ernie, in the chest cavity. It progresses in an orderly way from one lymph node region to the next. This process may be slow or very aggressive. The disease typically spreads downward from the initial site. At the time of Ernie's diagnosis, the disease had already spread past his diaphragm to his spleen and eventually progressed to his liver and bone marrow. It follows a relentlessly progressive and, in those days, ultimately fatal course.

While the exact cause of Hodgkin lymphoma is unknown, doctors believe it may be primarily genetic. The cancer is caused by the mutation of cells in some genes in the body. When these cells mutate, they actually allow the normal cells to grow in an uncontrolled manner. In addition to the genetic cause, there may also be an environmental risk. For example, people who are exposed to certain chemicals, in particular solvents or pesticides, may have an increased chance of suffering from Hodgkin lymphoma. There was no evidence at the time to suggest that Ernie possessed either the genes or the environmental factors to cause his disease.
(Note: Seventy years after Ernie's death, his second cousin and Carrie's grandson, John, died from Hodgkin lymphoma.)

There are four stages of Hodgkin lymphoma. In Stage 1, only one group of lymph nodes is affected. In Stage 2, two or more groups of lymph nodes on the same side of the diaphragm are affected. By Stage 3, lymph nodes on both sides of the diaphragm are affected, and by Stage 4, other parts of the body besides the lymph system have been affected. We don't know where Ernie was at the time of his diagnosis, but by the end of his letters, it's clear that he had reached Stage 4. Once a person reached Stage

4, there was, at that time, no chance of being cured. Ernie felt better after each treatment because the treatment reduced the tumors, but it couldn't stop the progression of the disease.

Often the initial diagnosis of Hodgkin lymphoma is made by the patient. In Ernie's case, the discovery of a swollen lymph node in his neck, accompanied by backaches and the vague symptoms of a weak appetite and the lack of energy, led Sven to take Ernie to see Dr. Berge, who performed a biopsy, which yielded the presence of Reed-Sternberg cells that are specific to Hodgkin lymphoma. The results were sent to the hospital at the University of Minnesota for further examination, and Dr. Berge's preliminary diagnosis was confirmed.

From the 19th century until the early 1930s, treatment for Hodgkin lymphoma ranged from palliative care to surgery, arsenic and other natural compounds. The treatment then underwent an evolutionary process that has turned Hodgkin from a fatal disease into a highly curable one. For Ernie, that process began in 1932 with radiotherapy—the use of high-energy rays for the destruction of malignant cells—which was, at the time, considered to be the first breakthrough treatment for Hodgkin lymphoma.

Ernie had radiotherapy treatments every other day. He would lie very still under a machine that first took x-rays so the doctor could mark where to give the treatment and then administered the radiation treatment. The idea was to kill the most cancer cells while missing as much healthy body tissue as possible. Unfortunately, that did not happen most of the time; the apparatus used to administer high amounts of radiation invariably killed healthy tissue as well as cancer cells, and most patients did not survive the disease. Even though it appeared that the doctors took great care to treat only the regions they knew to be involved in Ernie's case, the treatment killed or hurt healthy lymph tissue, which caused some of his pain. It would be another 30 years before the radiation treatment was sufficiently refined and advanced to save lives.

There were probably experimental forms of chemotherapy around in the 30s, but it wasn't until after World War II that chemotherapy drugs were developed. The first successful use of the drugs to fight cancer didn't occur until the mid-50s. Interestingly, one of the first effective chemo treatments for Hodgkin lymphoma involved the same chemicals used in mustard gas in the war.

The 1960s and '70s brought about two advancements in the treatment of Hodgkin lymphoma patients. The first was the shrinking of the radiation field so that only the involved nodes would get the radiation therapy, and the second was the use of a combination of chemotherapy drugs, which had been found to be highly effective, even in providing cures for advanced Hodgkin. For a while, radiation therapy alone was used to treat early stage Hodgkin, and chemotherapy alone was given to treat advanced stages of the disease. Eventually, it became standard practice to give both radiation therapy and chemotherapy to all patients—regardless of the stage of the disease—to try for a cure.

There is no question that if Ernie could have received the state-of-the-art treatment for his disease that is available today, his chances of survival would have increased from the "one in a million" that Dr. Berge gave him in 1932 to the 80% to 90% that patients today can expect. Ernie fought for his life with the best treatment available at the time. Sadly, it wasn't enough.[3]

June 2, 1932
Dear Pop and Brothers:

I'm getting along fine and I suppose it's getting along with you also. I write quite often because I have nothing else to do. But I know that it's rather hard for you because you are so busy. Please tell Fat and Ock to write a few lines. Just a few so I can see how they are getting along. What kind of farm work are you doing now? Have you seeded the barley? What about a barn roof, is that on also? In the sewing machine lays my knife. Please let it lay. You guys can use it but I want you to take care of it. My gun also. Please! Fat, I'm trusting you. I don't think it will be so awful long before I come home to you if it's God's will. After the 5th treatment the doctors looked at the gland. My! How small it is. Dr. Large said: "Well, Sonny, we'll soon fix you up so you can go home." I was glad to hear that. Dr. Bergland is chief of clinic. Dr. Johnson is assistant chief. And they come around to investigate about every week. We have a beautiful room overlooking the Mississippi. I sit on the window sill and gaze across the river. On the other bank is three more hospitals. The St. Thomas, St. Maries and Fairview, all Catholic too. There's one trouble with me and that is that I am so lively I can't sit still. I wander up and down the halls visiting other rooms, etc.

I visited Tom but he wasn't feeling too good. His sickness is a lot worse than mine but he still wanted to talk so I stayed. It's a sad story for Tom. He saw his father cry when he couldn't find a job. I guess he tried to get a job at Sears but there was to many people wanting that job. They had to live with relatives because they lost their house. His mother didn't want him to leave but his dad said that he probably should go. It's really tragic. Tom rode trains all over the country so he could find jobs. He rode on top of trains that had detectives who were so mean they would kick Tom off for no reason. He even got beat up once and he knew a guy who got his leg cut off because he fell under the train wheels. He told me about the time he was with another guy and they was going through a tunnel. He was scared because of all the black smoke that was in the boxcar so they crawled to the top of the train. The other kid got real sick. Boy, he's sure had a lot of adventures but that don't seem to be a good way to live, he was hungry and cold almost all of the time.

It's to bad Mom didn't get a ride with them people, because the turkeys won't live so good without her. By the way, how many turkeys have hatched already? I hope you have good luck with them. If I come home will you guys do me a favor. Promise not to laugh at my weight or size because I sure am skinny. I betcha Fat's taller than

I am now. But that can't be helped, after a few years I'll start growing. I don't mind if I'm small. Health is the main thing and I've got it now.

Do you guys have much fun? Has Ocky been out hunting for a "slasher" lately? I suppose they're getting their young now so its not for hunting. I talked with a man that had over 150 grown pigs! That sure is a lot of pork, but it won't bring him much money because the price is so low. I betcha Ocky is bending over the mirror this very minute. That's just a joke so don't take it to heart. Do you see Eddy much nowadays? I'll bet he is "drieving" with the girls. How is the pasture now? I'll bet it's a green carpet. Is my cat pulling in any gophers lately? Please preserve the small kittens. I would like to see them when I get home. Will you write and tell me all about the farm affairs when you get time? And I would like to have Fat and Ocky write also. Is Mamie still your cook? I bet she is an expert by this time. She is a good little girl. Mom said she is always willing and I agree with her. Maybe you have noticed the change in writing. That is because I have changed positions. Well, I suppose I must stop writing or you will faint because its just trash. But read it and write back as soon as you get time which I hope will be soon. I will close with love to all. From Ernie.

(Note: Ernie uses quotation marks to denote a non-English word. "Drieving," however, is not a Scandinavian word, at least not standard Norwegian or Swedish. It could be slang.)

Hodgkin lymphoma most often affects young people, so special attention needs to be paid to the impact of the illness and its treatment on their lives. One gets the impression from his letters that Ernie was largely ignorant of his disease—what it was and the truth about how he was going to be treated for it. The fact that he never uses the word "cancer" indicates that he either didn't know Hodgkin lymphoma was a kind of cancer, or the doctors never used the word to identify his illness, or he was afraid to use the word. I can understand a doctor's reluctance to explain to Ernie the dangers of the radiation therapy he would be receiving, since there was no alternative treatment. It would serve no purpose for a fifteen-year-old boy to know that the machine he lay underneath every other day was shooting high amounts of radiation on areas that the doctors believed contained affected lymph nodes, and that the treatment at first would make him feel better but over time would probably make him sicker because his healthy tissue was being destroyed along with the cancer cells. But I wonder if Ernie had any realistic expectations. I also question the wisdom of his doctors who kept reassuring him that they would fix him up so he could go home soon. Was so little known about the nature of Hodgkin lymphoma at that time that they actually believed Ernie could be cured, or were they indeed aware that the treatment was mostly palliative and were only trying to reduce his anxiety for the time being? Then there is the possibility that Ernie knew the reality of the situation but glossed over it in favor of presenting a rosy picture to his parents and brothers so as not to worry them. He was so worried about the distress his illness was causing his family that he almost always played down his personal distress, which begs the question: Did Ernie have sufficient emotional support from his aunt and uncle, hospital doctors and nurses, and his family to alleviate his anxiety?

Children, and even young adults, today rarely receive radiation therapy because radiation interferes with the normal growth of tissue and bones, preventing a child from reaching his full height and muscle density. Ernie, however, had no choice about radiation therapy; it was the only treatment available in 1932. Given that limitation, the doctors probably felt there was no valid reason for Ernie to adopt realistic expectations about his treatment and prognosis; knowledge about the reality of his disease could only lead to despair and loss of hope. There is also the question of whether the doctors should have been more forthcoming to Ernie's caretakers, his aunt and uncle, so they could have made the most informed decisions about his care as possible. But maybe they were forthcoming, and John and Carrie cared for Ernie the best way they could. At the very least, shouldn't Ernie have been made to understand radiation therapy so that he wouldn't continue to believe that the treatments were "electric," a belief he used as an explanation for his pain, which he never attributed to the progression of his disease? Perhaps not, for it was partly this belief that continued to allow him to hope... .[4]

About two weeks after Ernie entered the hospital, the doctors called his Uncle John to find out that Hedvig had gone home on the train. When Ernie heard, he understood the reason for his mother's abrupt departure but was devastated nonetheless. He almost made it seem as if Hedvig didn't say goodbye, but it's unlikely that was the case. It's more likely that he omitted from his letters any mention of a goodbye.

A few days later, the doctors came around and told him that he was through with his treatments and he had "gotten well" so fast that he was "almost cured." They sent him home to live with John and Carrie for a while. Ernie could hardly wait to tell his family the good news.

The big gland is so small as my little fingernail, the glands farther up are almost entirely dried up, and I feel as good as anybody. I have a good appetite and I am on the road to recovery. I hope this makes all of you happy because I'll soon be with you. On July 11, I am going back to the hospital because they want to see how everything turned out. Everybody, no matter how well they are, is ordered to come back to the hospital and see results. I am going to be out in the sun as much as possible because I want to be tan. Mom, please don't worry about me now, because I am just as well off as the rest of you. God has taken mercy and helped me along. In other words, I can just as well call myself well. Uncle John talked to Dr. Beecham and Dr. Large and they said that I am in fine shape, and that I was getting along just fine. John asked them if they thought I would get well and they said, "Why certainly!" Wouldn't that dump you over? Boy! I sure am happy. I had six treatments all together and that's a complete treatment. I sure wish I was back on the farm, because to me, there is nothing as nice as the farm. There is always the fresh pure air, and the smell and lure of the woods that I like best. I keep thinking about Tom. I hope he will get well to.

Ernie was both fascinated and baffled by Tom's life—or at least Tom's descriptions of his life. He couldn't conceptualize a way of life that was so different from his own. Tom regaled him with stories of his trip to New York City with his parents. Even though he must have been young, he talked about speakeasies, cellars, lounges, rib joints, and the like as if he had experienced it all firsthand. As Tom tells it, his parents took him to Harlem (*"people from all over the world go there..."*) which was swinging in the late 1920s and early 30s. *Tillie's Chicken Shack* with fried chicken and sweet potato pie; the *Plantation Club* which opened in 1930 to compete with the *Cotton Club*, (and whose owner was found dead two nights later.... *"They even wrecked the place and threw things outside!"*); the *Hot Peanuts Man's* cart; *Loft's Candy Shop*—Ernie listened to Tom's stories about all of these places. One story bothered him. It was about Tom's parents going to a famous theater where they saw great musicians such as Louie Armstrong play and sing. Tom told Ernie that there were mostly black people in that theater because *"they can't go to theaters that were just for white people. They weren't allowed. Something about that don't seem right."*

Tom's a city boy, he says that Chicago is the best place in the world. He even talks about places in Chicago that I aint never heard of like "speakeasies" and supper clubs and theaters. But to me, it is no contest. Before I left the hospital he told me so many stories it made me feel dizzy.

Here is one story, it's pretty interesting. Some guys were riding in the boxcars and all of a sudden it stopped in the middle of the night. One of them railroad detectives woke them up and told them to get out. A guy decided to run for it but he didn't make it, the "bull" shot him, he didn't hit him but he beat up the guy bad. Those "bulls" are mean, they line the hoboes up to the cars and hit them over the head with a blackjack and they swear at them. One time a mean "bull" told a bunch of young guys to get off the train and he robbed them of all their money. A couple of guys were working the fields and had a few dollars they was going to send home but it was all taken. One guy had four dollars to his name and the "bull" took two dollars for his ticket. Some of the kids he met on the road really had hard lives.

I think that Tom is a lot sicker than me. I like getting letters from my Mom, Pop, and bros. and he doesn't get hardly any. His Mom writes him a letter once in a while, she must know how sick he is but he seems so sad and homesick. He really misses his mother. Sometimes he talks like he's bragging and tough but I think he's pretty scared. He even cries sometimes. When you come to pick me up in July, I hope you'll bring him some of Laling's homemade bread and homemade potato soup. Say Mom, do you know the Montgomery Ward catalogue we order from. Tom used to go to the store in Chicago.

When I get back I mean to make myself useful. I might not be able to do so much at first, but when I gradually gather strength, I will be as hard as a brick. There is hardly any flesh on me, but what there is is all muscle. I'll bet you guys are strong as oxes by now, including Fat and Roy. By the way, how is the little "busy bee?" He sure was busy when I was up there.

And above all, how is my cat? Please take good care of her and Fat, let this be a warning. Don't toss her in the tank and half drown her. How is my calf? I hope he is growing. Mom do you know that man in the hospital in our room with the pipestem legs? Well, he's getting worse and worse and still he swears. I'll soon be with you now and I sure am glad. I will close with love to all. Ernie. Please write back, you too Fat and Ock.

Ernie was a good-looking kid, with light brown hair and blue eyes. He was five feet eight inches tall, with a slim build—"wiry" everyone said—and possessed a temper which flared up whenever he perceived an injustice being perpetrated on himself or on others. He had a "fighting aptitude," according to his brother Raymond (Fat), and fought a couple of times a week when he went to school in Minneapolis, mostly because someone was always trying to get the best of him but also because he enjoyed winning.

Fat was rotund with an insatiable appetite and an even temper that allowed him to defer to Ernie in most instances of disagreement. They were close friends, partly because of their age and partly because of their mutual interest in hunting and all things related to the woods. However, while Fat loved hunting, Ernie was passionate about the sport. He always wanted Raymond to go hunting with him. One day Fat wasn't in the mood so he refused. Ernie wouldn't take no for an answer. "You fat bastard, you come with me or I'll knock the wind out of you." Raymond went. What's particularly amazing about this exchange is that Ernie most likely already had some of the general symptoms of Hodgkin lymphoma, e.g., a lack of appetite and fatigue, but they didn't decrease his desire for hunting.

Ernie was street smart and did surprisingly well in school, endearing teachers to him even though he barely tolerated their interference in his life. (A comment on one of his report cards for the seventh grade read: "Ernie has a hard time sitting still in class and this prevents him from absorbing much of the information that is being taught.") It's probably a testament to his charm that he left the Minneapolis school system in good stead with his teachers and even with most of the kids he beat up at some point during his career.

When Sven moved his family to the farm in northern Minnesota in 1930, Ernie needed one more year of school before he was allowed to end his education. He completed eighth grade in a little one-room schoolhouse on the corner (School District 112), which was heated in winter by a wood stove and featured an outhouse located a far distance from the classroom. The teacher, who wasn't much older than some of the students, either rode a horse to the school or walked. With either mode of transportation, she had to arrive early enough to start the fire in the morning and pump water into a drinking bucket. At the end of the day, she swept the floors and wiped off the desks. She did all of this in addition to teaching eight grades in one room. As she taught one grade, all of the other students heard the lessons. Ernie's memories of school dealt mostly with the games they played in the woods during recess.

It was just Raymond and Ernie who went to school together, the older boys having finished in Minneapolis and Roy not yet old enough. Raymond was in the sixth grade and happy to be in school with Ernie, who was his best friend. Ernie quickly established his fighting reputation, and Fat was a willing ally.

He said that Ernie would regularly beat the stuffing out of the Lind brothers on the way home from school every day, sometimes with very little provocation. In fact, the brothers expected it to happen and just tried their best to minimize the damage. Amazingly, there were no lasting hard feelings between the Pearsons and the Linds, at least none that could be attributed to their boys' daily altercations.

In those days, almost everyone who lived in the country went to the eighth grade and then graduated. Those who wanted a high school education had to go to Roseau, but hardly anyone did. The Superintendent of the County Schools, Charlie Christianson, tried to change this pattern and even made a trip out to the farm to convince Sven and Hedvig that they should send Ernie to high school. His argument was that the Pearsons and their neighbors were foolish not to send their kids to high school because they could get the roads plowed and maintained if they did so. What he didn't realize, I guess, is that not many people had cars and there were no busses, so plowed roads were not necessary, a situation that created little incentive to further their children's education.

Ernie and Fat had a lot of fun on the farm during those two years they were together. They were inclined to engage in more than a little mischief. Sometimes they took the horse and toboggan to school on winter mornings, and on those occasions they would stop at Mr. and Mrs. Selvig's house to warm up before school. Selvigs always insisted that they have a little lunch but the boys had a hard time eating there because the animals lived right in the house and there was no fresh air. True to their natures, Ernie would decline the invitation while Fat was not quite able to resist the good food, so he would eat both his and Ernie's, rationalizing that they didn't want to hurt their hosts' feelings. One morning, Ernie kept sneaking his food to the little pigs that were nearby and Fat, not noticing, couldn't understand why Ernie wasn't getting full. Mrs. Selvig, on the other hand, was delighted with the boys' appetites for her food that morning.

Another time, Ernie and Raymond singlehandedly got a neighbor drunk in the middle of the afternoon, while he was drinking coffee at their house. Sven and Hedvig took in anyone who didn't have a place to live during those hard economic times. One of the homeless they helped was a bachelor named Mr.

Watkins who slept in the summer kitchen for a few months, until he found a place to live. One afternoon, feeling bored, Ernie and Raymond got their hands on some moonshine (the circumstances of how they did that are unclear). They managed to dump quite a substantial amount into Mr. Watkin's coffee cup. Mr. Watson kept trying to correct the taste by adding sugar. When his behavior started reflecting an inebriated state, especially when he called Hedvig his "sweetie pie," Ernie and Raymond had to own up to what they had done.

Ernie remembers only the fun and happy times of his years on the farm. He and his brothers had the whole outdoors as their world. They felt unburdened. Sven and Hedvig provided solid, practical commonsense guidance in their sons' lives, and everyone performed the chores and executed the obligations that make a family and a farm work. Ernie loved everything about the farm, including the intimate contact he enjoyed with the animals. Interacting with them was second nature to him. He fed and watered the animals, played with them, petted them and assigned them names, e.g., Sir Potley. This close relationship with the animals not only immensely enriched Ernie's experience on the farm, but it likely made him a kinder, more empathetic person. It most certainly made him sick with yearning for the animals he had left behind on the farm that he loved.

June 5, 1932
Dear "Laling" and the rest.

I am just writing a few lines to let you know how I am getting along. I don't want you to worry one bit about me because I am coming along o.k. We should have sent this letter earlier, but the night before last John forgot it, and last night we went fishing. We caught 25 fish, 7 bullheads and the rest sunfish and perch. We fish right off the shore. John uses hip boots and tonight he is going to bring me home a pair of them so I can wade way out to. I caught quite a big fish. How goes the hunting and fishing with you? Have you got any more "slashers?"

I saw Tom today. I found out that he came here from California where he was working with vegetables and oranges. I think he was planning to work in the fields here when he got sick. The saddest thing is that he wasn't paid much not even enough money to send home to his family. On one job he made 20 cents an hour and worked 12 hours a day, then he could send some money home but that didn't last long. Once he worked all day and the guy wouldn't pay him, just fruit. He sure knows how to catch a train when it's moving. And he aint afraid either. He can grab a boxcar doing 25 miles per hour. He says you run alongside it and you get one hand on the handle, then you run some more and swing yourself around and get two hands on the handle. Then you lift your foot up and push the train. But he says it don't work right all the time and it's easy to lose your grip. He knew one kid that lost his grip and was nearly killed. But it must have been great to hear that train whistle, that would be a good thing. He said they had to catch the trains at night and when the train was moving because of the "bulls" that were so mean. They carried lanterns and rifles they use to beat the hobos. I don't know much but I don't think he should just ride trains without any place to go, just riding around the country looking for food. I sure don't understand that. He had a good friend who was riding the trains with him but he thinks something happened to him. He said that the depression causes people to ride trains because they don't have any jobs.

How is "Laling" and Pop? I hope they are feeling fine. And how are you kids? I for myself am getting along pretty good. I have pain once in a while but not much. How are the cattle and horses and chickens and also the turkeys? I bet the turkeys are growing. Have you had any rain up there lately? I sure hope so.

About that coming down here before the time is up, I don't know. I think it's foolishness on my part because it's just a waste of time and money. Wait until July and then come! I may have to stay and take more treatments but I don't mind because when I come home I will be o.k. So don't worry. I made a little cart for the kids today just for the fun of it. Ha! Ha!

I will close with much love to all. From Ernie. P.S. Write soon please. Tom said to greet you. He wishes he could have some of your potato soup, "Laling."

(Note: "Laling" must have been an affectionate term for Ernie's mother. It is not a Scandinavian word.)

The 1930s was one of the most downbeat times American has endured. "It was more than a lack of understanding. It was an aimless, disembodied feeling, as though the world had disappeared. The same feeling you have during an earthquake that's beyond your control."[5]

The Great Depression affected everyone, except the wealthiest people who were not ruined by the stock market crash on October 29, 1929. In the city, millions of people were out of work—day laborers, insurance salesmen, steel workers, business owners— and by 1932, only one fourth of those unemployed families had received any relief. People lost their homes and were forced to live in unfit environments, with houses made of cardboard and other scrap materials. City street corners were crowded with poor people selling apples for five cents. Children ate lard sandwiches and tucked cardboard into their shoes to cover holes to keep the water out. The unemployment and food lines grew longer every day. A sense of hopelessness and despair marked the faces of people who stood in long lines for a stale crust of bread and watery soup.

Tom described depressing Chicago scenes to Ernie, such as men fighting over garbage that had been set in back of a restaurant. They were digging in garbage dumps either to feed themselves or their children off the leftovers from wealthy people who could still afford to eat well. He said that he saw old people wearing clothes with holes and held together with safety pins. He also related what Ernie called a *sad situation*: a friend of their family who couldn't afford to use his car so he jacked it up on blocks after having taken the battery out and oiled the cylinders and then removed the wheels.

While the Great Depression affected everyone in the whole country, it was the hungry and starving children who wrenched the lives of compassionate people still able to maintain a comfortable lifestyle. Many had to drop out of school because they had no shoes and warm clothing for the winter months. The school rule was that children could go barefoot until the first frost. At that time, they either had to wear whatever shoes were available—even second hand boots so big they could hardly walk in them—or stay home. Tom told Ernie that the rich kids in Chicago wore elegant sweaters and were driven to school in fancy cars, while the poor kids wore old shoes with no socks, causing raw and swollen ankles. Many stayed home out of shame. The poor farm kids fared no better. In fact, schools in rural districts were so hard hit that a significant number of them closed altogether.

While life was not easy in Salol, Minnesota at that time, most families survived with intractable faith in God, strong family ties, and hard work. For farmers, such as Sven and Hedvig, it appeared that the Great Depression didn't change their lives much. And when they did feel the strain of poverty, they carried on as they always did by "cutting corners" and "making do."

The collapse of wheat prices, however, marked the beginning of a stressful time for farmers. Between 1930 and 1931, farm prices fell more than 30 percent. Then, in 1931, U.S. wheat crops broke all records—a bumper crop— but the supply forced the price down, so many farmers went broke and had to abandon their fields, as banks foreclosed on their mortgages. By 1932, farmers were drowning in debt and facing foreclosure for back taxes. And it wasn't just wheat that had sunk below the cost of producing it—milk, cattle, and hogs were in the same depressed situation. To make matters worse, the dryness of those years—which turned out to be an eight-year drought—made any kind of farming difficult.

Ernie worried about the abnormally light rainfall and the effect it was having on the crops; the corn especially was in danger of drying out. *"I'm praying for rain for the farmers, but all it does is rain in the city."* As if the dryness and low prices weren't enough, grasshoppers invaded Minnesota fields and destroyed them in hours, consuming paint off the houses along the way.

American farmers, the bastion of stability, could have succumbed to the anger and sadness that enveloped the country during this heart-wrenching time and just given up the fight. Some did and were forced to join other homeless who roamed the country in hopelessness and despair. Tom told Ernie about a friend of his father who lost his whole farm and had to leave his family with relatives while he rode the trains looking for work. All he carried with him was a picture of his wife and children. But most farm families were indomitably attached to their land, so they focused on all of the things that they could count on—simple home-cooked meals and time with loved ones— not the things they didn't have. They did what they could to deal with the day in and day out adversity.

Perhaps it is true what they say about this hard time: People learned lessons that helped them to emerge from this period stronger than when they started. They had to be resilient and resourceful. They had to be selfless and reach out to one another. They had to swallow their pride and ask for help, a step that was hard to take for men who always prided themselves on being able to take care of their families. They even had to accept the role reversal of their children working to make money for the family and resist the temptation to not walk away because the humiliation was too much to bear.[6]

Why were Hedvig and Sven—and neighbors such as Rosalyn and Art Clasen—able to keep their farms going? A key factor in their ability to do so was money. They didn't have to borrow money to buy their land and equipment, so they had no bank payments and little risk of losing everything through foreclosures and bankruptcy sales. While farm after farm was auctioned off as large farm surpluses drove down prices, Sven and Art kept theirs. While people were leaving their farmlands because farms cost too much to maintain and were moving to places where there were big factories that offered employment, Sven and Art stayed. They knew what to do and how to grow in hard times. They provided for their families through hard work, just as they had always done. The Pearsons and the Clasens were almost totally self-sufficient: vegetable gardens; fruit trees (plums, chokecherries, pincherries); berries (raspberries, strawberries, blueberries); cows (milk and meat); and pigs, turkeys and chickens (meat and eggs). The only things they had to spend money on were coffee, sugar, salt, flour, cloth and kerosene. There was also the Watkins man who was happy to meet their remaining needs with products such as vanilla.

So Ernie's family carried on during the Great Depression. They hauled water, milked cows, fed the chickens and pigs, gathered eggs, pitched hay, picked corn, cranked the cream separator, cooked meals on a stove that burned wood, and heated water on the stove to take baths and wash clothes. They grew many acres of corn, wheat, rye, flax and barley. They grew bigger gardens to produce a hundred quarts of canned fruits and vegetables, which filled their cellar, along with potatoes, cabbage, carrots and more vegetables. They fished and hunted.

Yes, Ernie's letters recounted only happy times of his years on the farm, but the reality is that they *were* mostly happy times. It never occurred to the Pearsons—and their neighbors—to think of farming as a hardship; they simply believed in hard work so, during the Great Depression, they just worked harder. This is not to say that there weren't anxious times. For example, Ernie talks about how Sven was worried when milk got down to five cents a quart—also when the rain didn't come and the crops didn't grow or when a cow died. But no one in their house ate lard sandwiches or went to bed hungry. No one had to tuck cardboard into his shoes to cover holes in order for his feet to remain dry on rainy days. At the same time, there was no money for travel so no one came to visit Ernie all the while he was in the hospital.

June 7, 1932
Dear Pop, Mom, and Brothers:

I am writing a few lines to let you know how everything is coming along. I have been feeling fine, till just yesterday. First I was sick to the stomach. That lasted for a day and next morning it left me, only to be replaced by pains in my right leg. I was wondering over all this, when Miss Eaves called up and asked if the treatments was making me sick. She solved the questions for us, because we never knew what it was until she told us. I am feeling much better today. I feel perfectly well except for a few pains in my leg. Ho hum! I hope you are all getting along fine.

I would give my gun, watch and my $1.25 cent knife if I could be with all of you on the farm. Boy! That would be nice. Fat, you are my brother but my best friend to so I look up to you a lot. Now don't get a big fat head you aint that perfect. But we have a lot of fun together.

By the way, are you sure you sent that knife or are you just fooling. If it's really true then I sure am glad. Aunty says it cost only 5 or 6 cents to send a package like that because she used to send heavy packages of handkerchiefs and it cost only 3 or 4 cents to send it. There would be no word how glad I'd be.

I sure got a nice Mom, Pop, and Brothers. I am glad to know that you think so much of me. There would be nothing I like better than to get the knife. Of course, it's all up to you. I sure would like to have a squint at the knife. If you want to send it you can and if you don't want to you don't have to. But I sure wish you would do it. When I go back to the hospital I may have to take a few more treatments. But I don't think I have to.

In the meantime I am getting along o.k. I help Aunty with the dishes. She sure has a hard time to make the kids do something. I hope my brothers aint that way.

I wish I was home so I could carry water and do the dishes for "Laling." Do your duty, Fat. Help Mom all you can. Not that I'm perfect. But help her anyway. How are the crops getting along? We had quite a rain yesterday, and I hope it rained up there also. Have you planted my garden, Mom?

When I get back I'll bet it will be growing good. When I think of the farm I can hardly sit still. Every morning about 6 o'clock I sit down by the window and think over all the adventures I have had on the farm. I hate the city and I love the farm. I'm a regular storyteller. I tell them kids a hunting story every night.

We was down to the park one afternoon and we was not there 5 minutes before Kenny got into a fight with a kid pretty near twice as big as himself. They advanced toward each other. Suddenly Kenny made a movement and in an eyewink the big kid was on his back. Kenny kept him there until some other kids came and begin to pile on Kenny. The last thing on earth I'd want to do, would be to fight. But when I saw half a dozen kids on Kenny I began to upset them. All I done, was to shove them backwards until they quit beating on Kenny. Then we went home. Sunday we all took a ride out in the country but we had to go back because the grip got Aunty. John had it to. Elaine has still got the whooping cough and she coughs for 15 minutes in one straight line every half hour. She can hardly get her breath. Mom, will you do me a favor? Either you or one of the boys write, and when you do please let me know if I've had the whooping cough. Aunty wants to know because if I haven't had it I may get it and I wouldn't like that. But I think I've had it because I haven't got it yet, and I've been around Elaine quite a bit.

She got it from the kids across the street. It comes in spells. Mrs. King was down here yesterday and she asked how you was getting along. Gladys was down here too. She's a stuck-up little runt. She puts so much powder and lipstick on that she's just a mass of pimples. The little squirt!

We are going downtown today and do some shopping. This is John's day off, so me and Aunty and John are going downtown. John makes good beer but I never take none unless I got a bellyache. It takes away the pains.

There sure is an awful neighbor. Her name is Mrs. Ryan. She pretty near doused Kenny with a kettle of hot water on purpose. Then the old man ran after Orlin with a stick and nearly took his life.

I think I better quit because you guys will get tired of reading and besides the pencil is wearing out so I'll quit. With love to all. From Ernie. P.S. Please send my knife. Goodbye for the time being.

(Note: John and Carrie Pearson had six children: Harold, Kenneth, Orlin, Elaine, Virginia, and John.)

Ernie had his good moments when he was doing well and thought the treatments were working. And they were successful at first. But when new locations on his body were identified as having Hodgkin—and the disease kept spreading—it was all too much. Then the pain would start. Even when it was intense he attributed the pain to the effectiveness of the treatments. The most common general side effects of radiotherapy are reddening of the skin, tiredness, and loss of hair in the treatment area. None of these would cause Ernie to suffer from such severe nerve pain. Toward the end, his pain was caused by the progression of the disease, not by the treatment.

I am writing a few lines to let you know that I have some pain. Ha-ha that sure sounds goofy but its true. Mom, do you remember before you left that the Dr. told you the treatments would start to work on me? Well, Aunty called up the hospital and asked. The Dr. said the treatments would work on me and were bound to cause some pain. I was supposed to get some medicine for pain. Instead of having to wait in the hosp. Miss Eaves got it for us right away. Now don't worry about this here because them treatments are a great help to me. And don't forget that them treatments are electric and they are bound to cause some pain. But as soon as the pain is gone I am a new man again. The gland is still about as big as my fingernail. So you see, it sure has went down. Them treatments are working a little as the Dr. said it would. Please now "Laling" don't let this worry you because we will soon meet again. And I don't want Pop or brothers to worry about it either. There will be nothing better than to see my dear Pop and Mom and brothers again. Haven't you got rain up there yet? It sure is funny. Up there, where you need rain, you don't get it. Down here, where it can wait for a while we get plenty of it.

P.S. I asked Miss Eaves how Tom was doing. She said he wasn't doing so good.

(Note: Miss Eaves was a nurse, but it appears that she played an even more important role in Ernie's life— that of patient advocate.)

When an old tramp was asked by a teenage hobo how to get by without money, he replied, "Put your pride in your pocket, your hat in your hand, and tell them how it is."

(Note: I remember Uncle Raymond saying this when he talked about the Great Depression.)

As unemployment grew during the Great Depression, many adults became drifters and hobos in an attempt to find jobs so they could provide food for their families. When employment eluded them, their children were forced to try where their parents had failed—find jobs that would earn enough money to support themselves and send home. At the height of the Depression, 250,000 teenagers were riding freight trains. Boys and girls who should have been in high school and at home found themselves in boxcars and jungles. Some left home believing they were burdens to their families; others left because they were ashamed of the poverty that had enveloped their home. Desperate for food, they rode the rails looking for employment, sometimes to nowhere in particular and, at other times, traveling hundreds of miles on the chance of a job waiting for them at the end of the line, only to find that the job had already been filled.

"Your hunger really hurts," Tom told Ernie. "When there was no money and no way to get money, I'd go into a restaurant and order a glass of water.

I'd pour some ketchup in the glass and mix in soda crackers. All of the restaurants had ketchup and crackers on the tables."

They took to the roads. Where were their homes? Where were they going? How long had they been on the road? How did they live? What did they eat? Where did they sleep? What did they do all day? Some had been riding the trains for a couple of years, following the harvests that demanded hard work at starvation wages and sometimes no wages at all. Most though had been on the road for about 14 months and had travelled within a radius of only 500 miles. Tom had probably been travelling for a year—from Chicago to California and then to Minneapolis where he had to get help for his illness.

Homeowners and shopkeepers were generally sympathetic to the teenage hobos. They would invite them into their homes for a meal, give them a job to do, slide a dollar bill into their pockets, and send them to missions or churches for a night's sleep. While these acts of kindness helped the young people survive, they also made them feel even more homesick for their homes and families. When they went back on the road, waiting for a train to carry them farther away, they once again were alone.

In large cities, the Salvation Army came to the rescue of the homeless who could always count on a bowl of soup and an army cot for the night, if they were willing to sit through sermons and listen to short prayers. Tom told Ernie that "sometimes those prayer services were pretty long but the banquet they served was worth the waiting."[7]

Don Snyder was fifteen or sixteen years old in 1931 and '32 when he rode the trains, mostly throughout Ohio in a search of food that would keep him from starving and also help his family who benefited from having one fewer mouth to feed. He watched for the trains from his house, which was located on a hill in Findlay, Ohio. A train coming from the south had to slow down because of the crossing and then stop right where he lived. When he heard two sharp blasts from a locomotive whistle and saw the train come rolling into view, Don would grab his coat and catch a ride on a boxcar. "No trick," he said, "just grab the steel handrails on the sides of the boxcar and swing in to it." The trick, really, was getting off a slow-moving train. "You had to jump off at the right time because once the train picked up speed you could hurt yourself."

He didn't care about the destination. Many times the train would be going to Lima and he would go and return in one day. At other times, he would catch the train that was going to Indianapolis or some other place farther away, and he would be gone for several days. In both cases, he was saving his parents the cost of having to feed him every day. Sometimes he slept in a boxcar in a rail yard only to wake up the next morning to find that the train had taken off with him inside. If he didn't like where it was going, he hitchhiked to a destination.

Those were hard times for the Snyders. They lived in a large house, but property was all they had. Don's father—who "never drank, smoked, chewed, or snored but didn't go to church"—had lost his job and couldn't find another. His mother was a Pentecostal who went to church a lot. She made poultices—a tobacco poultice for daytime ailments and bread-and-milk poultices for whatever ailed during the night—and sold them to people who believed they worked miracles. Don's parents didn't want him to ride the rails, but when he did it, his younger brothers and sisters had a better chance of eating.

The way Don tells it today, "It was a terrible way to live. It was rough and dangerous but there was also a mystical quality. The sound and moan of a whistle in the silent darkness echoing through the hills. The smell of the cars and the clicking of the rails. The ding, ding, ding at the crossings. The excitement of avoiding the bulls and brakies. The open praries, the mountains and the clear skies above you. For all the hardships, you sometimes felt a faint longing to hit the road again."[8]

Both Ernie and Tom reached adolescence during the Great Depression. They were children of the Roaring Twenties, but Ernie was too young to participate or even possess an interest in the activities that dominated Minneapolis culture at that time. His older brothers, however, took advantage of the loose lifestyle by developing relationships with some of what their parents thought of as unsavory characters while they lived in Minneapolis. Hedvig and Sven themselves must have remained pretty isolated from the glitzy era. They were largely unaffected when the stock market crashed in 1929 because they had no life savings to lose.

While Ernie didn't know much about the Great Gatsby lifestyle of the flapper era with its fast dancing and illegal drinking, Tom seemed to know it all. He loved to impress Ernie with his street-smart knowledge. He talked about the jazz bars in Chicago with such confidence that Ernie, at one point, was convinced that Tom had first—hand experience with prosperity.

Tom talked about if you had a wad of money in your pocket you could walk right into a nightclub and order a pint of whiskey inside a can. It cost $15 at the *club but you could buy it on the street for half that price. But the whiskey ain't inside a can. Tom called it a bootleg whiskey because it's illegal. He says the shows in Chicago go all night. He keeps saying that there's just no place like Chicago but he says that things are really bad there too. He says there are soup lines sometimes hundreds of people waiting in line to get some food. He knows about folks who sleep in shacks in little towns called Hoovervilles. Imagine sleeping in shacks made out of tin and cardboard boxes. I know we aint rich but the farm gives us everything we need. The city's not like that. John said there are people waiting in line for food here in Minneapolis. Tom thinks Chicago is the greatest place in the world and says I should go with him but I don't want to go nowhere except the farm.*

Tom talked almost as much about California as he did about Chicago, especially the "perfect weather." He told Ernie that he met farmers who had left home and were following the jobs—wherever crops were being harvested. There was some work, they said, especially in the new fields of cotton that were being planted, but it wasn't enough. Ernie had a hard time with the concept of farmers living in their trucks. *"It's a sad day when farmers lose their land."*

June 13, 1932
Dear Pop, Mom, and brothers:
I am feeling fine now and I wish you wouldn't worry about me. In Pops letter to John, Pop said that you couldn't raise money enough to come and get me.

If you come now then you are 1 month to early because I am going back for one day to the hospital to have them see how it will turn out on July 11th. Don't come until then. John is going to town today to buy writing paper. We been out of it for one day. 1,560,000 thanks for the beautiful knife you sent me. Also for the underwear. I don't know what to say I am so happy.

How are Mom and Pop getting along? I hope you are all fine and above all, don't worry about me! Especially you Mom. Take it easy and I'll soon be with you. And when I come I'll be entirely allright. If you come now it will take just twice as much money. So wait until July 11th. But Please, Please, Mom. Don't worry!

How are things going on the blessed farm? I hope the calves are growing. And the turkeys? What about them? I bet "Laling" is feeding and taking care of them. Aint that right "Laling."

Mrs. King was here one night for a visit. They received Eds letter and showed it to us. She said it was real good writing Ed. I guess they're going to take us out for a ride but I don't care much about that. Because John took us out for a fishing trip. We rented a boat and rowed all around. We caught only 8 that were of size. I rowed the boat all the way to shore. We're going out tomorrow again for croppies. I just wrote these few lines to let you know how I feel. And I am fine. I'll soon be with you again. Do you know that "dollar" you sent me? Well, its all saved because Aunty bought me a nifty pair of pants. When I get home then you can have the dollar, because I know how hard it is to get money. It will buy a few groceries if nothing else. Fat! Will you do me a favor?

Help Mom as much as you know how. You know how we always helped Mom and the big kids helped Pop. I'm not there now so you have to take over. When I get home we'll work together again. And we'll hunt. I'll even eat more because I have an appetite now.

Ocky was that a 30-30 you traded for or was it a 30-40. I know you got 2 bucks to boot. I bet you that came in handy. Ed said it was like one of these Kentucky rifles. But that don't matter as long as it can shoot. By the way how is my little rifle? Please take care of it guys because I worked hard for it.

Fat wrote and told me that he bored a woodchuck with it. Please take care of it guys, because even if you don't like it, I sure do. Write and tell me about all the hunts you guys take.

(Note: When Ernie was fourteen years old, he wanted a .22 rifle that cost only five dollars, but there was no money for such a purchase, so he picked blueberries to sell until he had enough to buy the gun. He also bought a box of ammunition that cost fifteen cents.)

And how is the "Little Weasel." I know he is getting along all right. John gave me a dandy haircut yesterday. Mom do you know my suit? Well Aunty is fixing the cuffs on them so they won't be so long.

Did I tell you that John took me to the hospital? He left me there for 2 hours. I asked Miss Eaves about Tom. She said he aint doing so good but I went to see him anyway. He was mighty happy to see me, seems he couldn't wait to tell stories. Boy, he's had an interesting life. Now this is what Tom told me today. He met 2 little boys last winter who almost froze to death riding underneath the train. They almost couldn't hang on to the bars any longer. I feel sorry for them, must have been scared out of their minds and they were only 9 or 10 years old to. Tom said that the boxcars were so cold in the winter that some of them hobos froze to death. He got real cold to but all of them in the boxcar took turns keeping everyone awake otherwise he would have froze to.

There was many people who were kind to the hobos. Tom said that one time the engineer slowed down the train to let him off so he wouldn't have to walk seven miles. Sometimes when Tom begged for food they would give him a sandwich and he could eat it on their back porch sometimes they let him come inside to eat with the family. One thing I liked that he told me was when he would go into a restaurant and always sit between two people and ask the waitress if there was jobs he could do for a meal. If she said no one of the people would tell the waitress to give him breakfast. I think that was pretty smart. Sometimes Tom had to go 2 days without eating and he didn't have clothes except the ones he left home with. I guess I'm really understanding the depression from Tom. I feel so sorry for him, he aint doing so good here either. I don't care if I see the country. Tom talks about all the places hes been but all I want is the farm. It's the best there is, it don't seem like we have a depression there.

Tom said he knew some Negro hobos too. They were treated way worse than the white hobos, people wouldn't give them food and made them sleep in barns with the cows. He saw one getting beat up when he couldn't run away from the "bulls." I guess all hobos aint the same. Them "bulls" would walk on top of the cars and on both sides so the hobos would be trapped. When they tried to run away, they was usually caught. Some of the hobos died in the boxcars or on the tracks. I wonder what they did with the bodies.

Do you know Tom can sing hobo songs and he sang one for me. I think the music gives him hope. But he sure knows a lot about what's happening in the country, I guess that comes from his travelling. He says it's really dry in Oklahoma and Texas and there are bad storms that blow dust all over. Are the crops okay on the farm? Or is it dry there to? He brags about Chicago something awful, keeps talking about how Chicago has great nightclubs that serve bootleg drinks, shows go on all night. He even says that Chicago ships the finest beer and liquor to New York.

Is Joseph still running his little place? And how are the crops? I sure hope you get rain. I been praying that some might come and I hope it will. Praying for a thing helps a lot. When I used to have pain in the hosp. I used to pray that it would leave me and it did. Do you know them people that wouldn't give you a ride, Mom? Well the lady has blood poison. I will close with love to all. From Ernie. Please write soon brothers. Goodbye.

(Note: This letter was written on a form, "Board of Park Commissioners Daily Time Report—City of Minneapolis.")

By far, the most popular mode of transportation for homeless transients, including hobos, during the

Great Depression were the passenger car blinds and the freight trains, described in detail in "A Hobo Memoir:"[9]

"The blinds were the spaces between baggage or passenger cars outside the accordion-like structure that surrounded the walkway between the cars. At the bottom of the car ends there was a narrow transverse platform or step that you could stand on. Then up the outer corner of the car there was a vertical railing or "grab-iron" as it was called, that you could hold on to. This put you in standing position looking out to the side enjoying the scenery as it flashed by. Riding the blinds was not all that dangerous so long as you stayed alert and did not loosen your hold. However, it was very tiring over long distances because you couldn't relax or sit down and have a cigarette as you might when riding the tops of freight cars or inside an empty box car. The advantage, of course, in riding the blinds on passenger trains was that wherever you were going, you got there a hell of a lot faster... . When the train started to move we sprinted up toward the front and swung up into the first blind behind the tender and we were on our way."

Hobos worked for their food: chopping wood, carrying water, weeding the garden—a half hour of completing tasks such as those would earn them a meal that they could take with them on the train. They liked to distinguish themselves from the tramps and bums: hobos travelled and worked; tramps travelled but didn't work; and bums didn't travel and didn't work. The distinction was often lost among the general population, however. Tom told Ernie, "If a guy doesn't have a job and he rides trains looking for work, he's called a bum or a hobo. I don't want to be called neither, but I don't have a job so I guess I'm both. It doesn't matter what you're called."

June 18, 1932
Dear Pop, Mom and brothers:
I thought I would wind up with a few lines to let you know how things are coming along. I hope you are all feeling fine. I am getting along fairly fine now and as time flys, I will soon be at the hospital again.

How are things coming along on the farm? How are the calves feeling? Is my little calf growing any? We went fishing Sunday and we caught only 8 fish. We went fishing last night at Twin Lakes and we caught 24 Sunfish and Perch. I met a boy about my own size and we started talking. I asked him if he lived in Robbinsdale and he said yes. I said Do you know Delkeens? He said Why that's me. I asked him if he was Marlin Delkeens and he said he was. Just think of it! I was talking to him and we didn't even recognize each other. Funny things can happen.

How is mom and pop feeling? Don't Worry about me Mom, because I'll soon be home. About that dollar you sent me. I spent 10 cents of it for fruit and I hope you don't get angry with me for it. I thought you wouldn't mind if I spent a little of it for plums and apples. I told you before that Aunty had bought me a dandy pair of pants and it didn't cost me a cent. John and Aunty sure are nice to me. John and me are going fishing about every night after he gets done with work. Aunty washes my shirts and I always have a shirt on my "roug." Sometimes she don't bake her own bread though. She gets it sliced from the store. It's called Wonder Bread, they gave us that in the hospital too. I sure don't like it, it tastes like paste. It ain't so good but it's sure easy for making sandwiches.

How are the kids? I bet Roy is "dreiving" with his slab-barns and houses. How is Fat? Why don't Fat and Ocky drop me a line when Ed writes. But I can't kick they sure been writing steady enough. I sure miss my brothers. A guy can meet all kinds of people. But theres nothing like family. My brothers are my friends especially you Fat. Because we are so close in age.

I want to thank you again for the knife I got. It sure was a dandy one. I been praying that rain would come and save the crops and I sure hope it does.

Has Ocky been hunting lately? I bet Fat is using the "life" out of my gun. I sure wish I was with you all up on the farm because to me there is nothing as nice as the Farm. How are you coming along Ed? Is that rheumatism in your wrist any better? I hope it is. I am sending you a picture of myself and some others that was taken 3 days after I came out of the hospital.

Please don't think I look that way now. I have a coat of tan on my face and arms. Please don't laugh at that picture. I know its awful but I look better now. Write more often Brothers and I will like it better. Ocky and Fat write to me because I sure like to hear what you guys write about. Do you go hunting "Slashers" anymore, Ock? Or is it to many weeds. Help Mom all you can Fat.

Will you? Wait until I get home, Mom, then I'll help you all I know how. I sure have changed since I left the Farm this spring. I can walk good now, and I have no pain except when the treatments work on me. The Dr. said they would cause some pain but I aint worrying about that. And I aint lonesome even if I have to take a few more treatments. Well I think I will close for this time. I send my love to you all. From Ernie. Please write soon. Don't worry Dear Pop and Mom.

Did Ernie know that he was supposed to maintain good nutrition, drink plenty of fluids, take it easy, and keep the skin in radiated areas dry? We only know that he had a lot of pain, in his legs and all over, and this he attributed to the treatment, not the disease.

The following is a letter that Carrie wrote to Hedvig in Norwegian and has been translated into English.

Dear Hedvig and Family—

I shall write a little more to you in Ernie's letter. We are all well enough, although a cough has taken baby Elaine, but it is almost over now. And Ernie is not so well now. I think he has hard pains in his back and stomach and in the thigh most of the time that last long and his appetite is poor. I gave him vegetable soup and egg nog for lunch but he threw it up and he said that his appetite is gone.

I have talked with Miss Evans and she said we should take him to see the doctor but it was hard to take him today so she said to give him his medicine with the "main dish." Poor Ernie. He had to sit so long today because he had such pain and it is my opinion that we should take him to the doctor on Monday. Miss Eaves is kind and wants to help him all she can.

I feel so sorry for Ernie that he has to suffer so much. And he's so good-hearted. He feels bad that he is sick for it bothers us.

We bought another box of American pills and the doctor said he should take them before bed but he sweats so much. I get up many times at night to watch over him.

Ya, Hedvig, maybe I shouldn't write so much but I have to speak as I see it. Ernie was so confident when he came home from the hospital.

He lies in his bed and thinks about something so he forgets his pain, so I say he's thinking about an ice cream he ate. Ya, well, when he becomes better he likes to be in motion so it will be pleasant to see him get well again.

Now I shall stop with many greetings to you from all of us. I do my best, Hedvig. Ernie is so worried about you he can't help himself.

Kindly, Carrie

June 21, 1932
Dear Brother Oscar:

So you downed a deer on the run! Well, I'll be jiggered! Ocky, you sure can shoot. Was you nervous or did you take it as easy as you did when you got the first one? I can't help but give you credit!

I bet you are just like me. I don't mean in shooting, but I mean in loving the woods. To me, I don't think there is nothing as wonderful as the woods. I know Fat feels that way to. We got that from Mom. She loves the woods a lot to. If I get well again, you will let me hunt with you once in a while, won't you? Remember this winter Ocky? We sure went hunting a lot didn't we? You and Fat and me. Ocky, if I was you I'd see how many deer I could get this summer. Do you think you will like your new rifle? Has it got good rifling? It's no matter what gun you get hold of, Ock, you can shoot good with them all. Isn't Ed hunting any lately? Ed can shoot pretty good to. What do you like best to do Ock? Still-hunt, post, or walk slowly along?

I asked John to take me to the hospital to see Tom. He couldn't talk much today, he was so weak. He talked a little about the gangsters but it was mostly stuff he said before. I don't know if it's all true. He was homesick to and even cried. He didn't want to quit school but had to because there wasn't no money for clothes or books or anything. He didn't want to leave home either but there were to many kids to feed so his father told him it would be all right to go. Tom sent some money home at first but then he couldn't find jobs that paid anything. Seems like he didn't have no good luck charm. He's pretty brave.

I wish he could have some of Laling's potato soup and her homemade bread too. I'm lucky to have John and Auntie.

Tom said he did some hitchhiking between train rides but he had a hard time getting rides because he was so dirty from the trains. He had the best luck at night when the cars couldn't see how dirty he was. He says that hitchhiking is harder than riding the trains. Boy, that kid has been all over the country!

How is my rifle, Ock? Is it in as good shape as when I left? I sure hope so. I just wrote these few lines in answer to the letter you wrote me, Ock. I sure am glad to hear that you got rain and that it looks like more. I am so pleased to hear it that I don't know what to do. How are all the rest of my brothers and Dear Pop and Mom coming along? Are you all feeling all right? I sure hope so. Aunty likes to hear from you folks so much that I let her read a few of the letters I get. Mom, maybe you could write to her a few lines now and then, little "Laling." She said she sure was an eater of Deer meat. But she wouldn't want you to send any because it's to risky. Of course I only told Aunty and John about the "slasher."

Aunty and I and John wouldn't think of telling the kids. So you Don't need to worry at all. I just wrote these few lines to the answer of your letter so I think I will close and write more next time. I am feeling pretty good. The treatments are working on me now. When I go back in July I may have to stay and take more treatments but don't let that bother you. With much love to Laling, Pop and the rest of my Brothers

Even in Ernie's naiveté and his fascination for Tom's life, he was incredulous about some of Tom's stories. For example, he was skeptical of Tom's account of the Lindbergh baby kidnapping (*how does he know these things?*) and the WWI veterans who had set up camps at the Capitol because the government refused to pay them for fighting in the war. *"Tom said there was a lot of commotion in Washington when some guys who fought in the War were trying to get their pay and some of them died. It sure is bad when the government won't give men who fought in the war the money they're supposed to have."* But it was Tom's obsession with criminals and his knowledge of their life stories that really impressed Ernie. Tom not only knew the criminals but also their turfs: Al Capone from Chicago, Bugsy Segal from Las Vegas, Bonnie and Clyde and Lucky Luciano from New York, and Pretty Boy Floyd from Missouri. Ernie told his brothers that the stories about the Chicago gangsters would *"make you guys faint dead away."*

Tom was especially obsessed with Al Capone who, between 1927 and 1931, was considered to be the ruler of Chicago: smart and cruel and loved by many. Poor people loved him because he paid them to make bootleg, and rich people loved him because they could drink it. Tom told Ernie that he was angry when Eliot Ness got Capone for tax evasion in 1931 and when Capone became incarcerated at the time of Tom's hospital stay. He relished telling Ernie about the St. Valentine's Massacre in 1929, when Capone's men gunned down seven rivals.

Another person who admired Capone was Anna Juliet Michelle who lived during that time, and four decades later wrote an article entitled *Capone, the Other Image*. She knew Capone as "Uncle Al" who lived three blocks from her house and was a benefactor to her family. Her father owned a garage where Capone had his car fixed and played card games with her. Anna described Capone as having a deep smile and crinkly grey eyes, with ears that he would wiggle for her. He showered her with several velvet dresses and a golden heart on a chain for Christmas when she was eight years old. During the Depression, Capone sent someone to her house on a weekly basis to give her mother money, while her father was absent for days at a time. There were six children and the money was welcomed.

When Anna was fifteen, she heard stories about Capone and crime that ran in the *Chicago Daily News* and the *Tribune*. Knowing Capone only as an affectionate man, Anna needed to know the truth so she went to see him and confronted him with the reports. He answered that he was a victim of society. Anna never saw Capone again. Her father died in 1942. In 1946, she learned that "Uncle Al" was gravely ill. When he died, she went to the cemetery and knew that she was at his grave when she read the words "Qui Riposa" on the headstone. "Reposa" means repose and it was the word that Al Capone had sent to her family when her father died.

There is a quote at the end of the article: "I must state that, due to some of his policies, we have all benefitted. Today, in most cities, we may be able to extract justice where, in the past, money talked—guilty or innocent. Though Alphonse Capone may not have been the boy next door or the one who delivered your newspaper, he was human… . Society created him to salve the conscience and grease the outstretched hand. He was the shipping boy of that era and, as such, a victim. Like a coin, there are two sides to almost every question, and to a man, another image."[10]

While Tom wasn't able to articulate his feelings about Capone with the same level of sophistication that Anna Michelle possessed, he surely would have agreed with her conclusions. At the very least he would have loved her story.

June 22, 1932
Dear Pop, Mom and brothers,

I received your letter today and I sure was glad to get it. I'll bet Mom is worrying herself gray over me. I sure hope she don't. Are they really going to make a new road to the sandridge? That's going to be real handy.

Have you been up on the ridge? And is there going to be any blueberries this year? I should think there would be some, because there was none last year. You haven't told me yet how many turkeys there is this year. I hope there is a lot of them. I am glad to hear that my calf is coming along fine and the crops. I sure hope you get more rain.

I got to thank Fat and Ock and Ed for writing to me so regularly. I also got to thank "Little Laling" and Pop for being so good to me and so patient with me.

How is little Roy coming along? I bet he's as tough as "struick." And how is "Potley?" Is he stuck between 2 trees in the "Spruce Grove?" Oh, that's right there aint no "spruce grove." I suppose I'm dumb but I sure don't know nothing about it.

Did "Laling" like it or didn't she? I know she likes the trees. I hope she isn't sad about that. I sure wish I was home but I'll have to wait until July 11, or even longer than that, because I may have to stay and take more treatments. But even if I do stay, believe me, when I go home I will be cured. And don't worry little "Laling," because with Gods help, I will get well. How are things "Rosing" up around our place? Do you go to Roseau very often? I heard in your letter that it had been raining hard in Roseau.

Did you get a shower also? I hope you get about ten showers. How much timothy did you seed in this year? I hope the Flax and the Barley picks up. It sure is tough when you have to haul the water. Fat, how is my little "Lucky?" Take care of it. And also take care of my garden, but I'll bet it won't amount to much without rain. If you don't get enough rain up there, everything will dry up. When you start haying be sure to hay enough, if you have time.

That's funny "Ralla" can't stop kicking. I bet the pasture is nice and green now. I hope the dry spell won't wreck it.

How is my "Fesk?" I bet she's dragging in gophers and rabbits all the time. Are the little kittens growing? Aunty received a portrait of Ruby. Did you get one to?

About them suspenders now. I don't think I need them, Mom. I have my belt loose so it don't hurt me any. Aunty sure likes to hear news from Roseau. I let her read my letters. She sure enjoys them. Is it all right, Mom?

The little baby has got the whooping cough. She got it from Elaine. I sure enjoy your letters guys. Please write Brothers. You too Fat. Much love to all from Ernie. Please write (all of you).

(Note: Lucky-rifle; Ralla-cow; Fesk-cat)

While there is no evidence to suggest that Ernie thought much about the meaning of life—or questioned the meaning of anything—during his treatment, he desperately wanted to survive in order to be with his family on his beloved farm once again. He was also accepting of God's will. For the most part, he was effusively optimistic, but did he really feel the optimism, or did he just project it so the family he loved so dearly wouldn't worry?

June 28, 1932
Dear Pop, Mom and brothers.

I am getting lonesome for home so I thought I would write a few lines to get in contact with you. I don't care what nobody says, but to me there is no place like home. Every day and night I think of the farm. I love it with all my heart and soul. If you compare the lousy city with the farm, the city is a mere dump. The reason I wrote this letter is because of the affairs of the hospital.

Miss Eaves called and said that when July 11 comes I will start to take my treatments but I won't stay in the hosp. I will take 6 treatments and I will take one every other day. In the meantime I will stay at Aunty's. It will take 12 days to take all the treatments. I will go to the hosp. every other day.

The prospects don't look so bad. Do they? The real trouble is this: How can I get there every other day? Aunty can't hardly go because of the baby. And she has the whooping cough. John can't go because of his work.

If I know the way, I'd go alone. You got to take two street cars. If you stayed up on the farm instead of coming down in July, then we'd save money, because of the extra trip in coming down here. It's tough, aint it? You can do what you want to. You can either come down here or else stay. It aint good that people have to choose between being with someone whos sick and saving money. I want my Mom and Pop to be here but there's no money. I can be by myself. It's all up to you, write and tell me what you plan to do.

It's no telling how many treatments I have to take. At least, some day I'll be home at the blessed farm again. I sure like it. What are you doing up there now? When do blueberries start? In the last letter you told me to write all about myself.

At least I'll be able to see Tom.

Well, there aint much to write. My face has a different color. It's tan now and so is my arms. I gained 5 lbs., since I came out of the hosp. I been trying to gain weight with that dollar. I bought bottles of milk and fruit and stuff until it was all gone. At least I spent it wisely. I bought something worthwhile. Do you know that a coke and a Baby Ruth candy bar costs 10 cents and a loaf of white bread costs 7 cents? I didn't buy no coke. But I bought bread for Aunty. I wished I could drink all the milk I wanted. O Boy! That's why I wished I was out on the farm. Plenty of milk.

Don't mention anything of what I said in the letters you write to me, because Aunty reads them. She likes to hear country news. She sure is nice though, Mom. Well, I guess I will close with love to all from Ernie. Please write soon. You too Ock and Fat. Thanks for the letters you write to me. God bless you all.

It is my opinion that the previous letter contains three of the most poignant lines in all of Ernie's letters: *It aint good that someone has to choose between being with someone whos sick and saving money. I want my Mom and Pop to be here but there's no money. I can be by myself.* The lines reflect a rare moment when Ernie succumbed to self-pity, an emotion he must have felt often but kept to himself. His honesty is heartbreaking. It also begs the question of how Sven and Hedvig were able to pay for Ernie's hospital expenses. There wasn't much by way of insurance for hospitals at that time. In fact, hospitals struggled to make ends meet. The bad economic times forced doctors to help those in need, and many treated people for free or took something in trade, e.g. food. People donated fruit to the hospital kitchen and nurses canned peaches and pears during the evenings. It appears that, in the age of pre-Medicare and Medicaid and even pre-vaccinations and antibiotics, doctors did what they could with limited resources and depended on folks to pitch in to provide health care.

(Note: It was during this time frame that two pioneer programs provided the basis for the Blue Shield Plans. Blue Cross was created in 1929 as a way for a small group of teachers in Dallas to finance 21 days of hospital care by making small monthly payments to the Baylor University Hospital. At the same time, the Blue Shield concept grew out of the lumber and mining camps of the Pacific Northwest. Employers who wanted to provide medical care for their workers arranged with doctors to receive a monthly fee for their services.)[11]

In an interview with Ernie's brother, Roy, he said that Sven most likely paid for Ernie's hospital care with cash installments. Like so many in their generation, Ernie's parents believed in hard work and disdained handouts. Charity forced upon them by Ernie's illness would have been an abomination, and they would not have accepted it.

July 3, 1932
Dear Pop, Mom and brothers.

It's a wonder I am trying to write now, because of the splitting earache I had last night. You musn't blame me if this letter is a little goofy. I had such an earache that I didn't know what to do. It's not very often I cry for pain but I did last night. This morning it eased off. God must have answered my prayer last night for relief. After that I wonder if I am going home. Anyway, I am writing a few lines to thank you for the dollar you sent me again. I also thank you for the very interesting letter you wrote me. Boy! I sure have a nice Pop and "Laling" and brothers.

But I don't think you should send me any money because it sure is scarse. I like to get a little money, of course, because it comes in handy. But Tom says the depression is really bad so I think it must be affecting farmers to. So don't send me any more money. You need it so bad on the farm.

I haven't spent any of this dollar yet, but I think I will buy a few things if that's ok with you. You sure are nice to me. I wished I could see you soon, or else come home, but I suppose the time will come. Are you coming down here July 11?

I suppose you know that I am going to take more treatments. Do you? I am going to take 6 more. It will take 12 days. After that I wonder if I am going home.

I will come some day. I have to go home to the place I love so much. I just got to be patient. It takes a great deal of patience. You used to tell me to be patient, didn't you Mom?

Ed asked me quite a few questions in his letter. I will answer as many as I can.

That gland is half-sized now, and under a few more treatments I think it will disappear. Next. Yes, I have some pain in my back as results of the treatments. Next. Yes, that medicine helped a great deal. Next. I sleep quite soundly and I have a pretty good appetite. Next. I feel ten times as strong now as I did when I was home. There! That's all the questions that Ed asked.

Is the hay drying out now? I sure hope it is. Do you think there will be enough hay this year? I am sorry to hear that the Flax and wheat aint coming along good. The Flax would come in handy in the fall. Are all of you in good health? I hope so. You aint getting any more headaches are you Mom? And how are you Pop? The kids I don't need to ask because they are writing me some good letters. Keep on, won't you? Well, there aint nothing to write about so I will close. With love to all of you. From me, Ernie. I am praying for help. God bless you all. Write soon.

(Note: In this letter, Ernie wrote a sentence twice: *After that I wonder if I am going home.* I believe this marks a significant moment when he is entertaining serious doubts about his healing. However, in the very next paragraph he says, *I will come someday. I have to go home to the place I love so much. I just got to be patient.* For Ernie there has to always be hope.)

Every day and night I think of the farm. I love it with all my heart and soul. The place that Ernie loved so much—where he felt safe, secure and alive—included a sturdy two-story house with a cellar underneath the kitchen floor and a stairway from the front room that led to a large divided room upstairs. Sven and Hedvig slept in the one bedroom on the first floor while Ernie and his brothers (and anyone else who was visiting) slept in the upstairs room, which featured a sloping ceiling with rafters and a window at each end. At one end of the kitchen, next to the cellar, was a pantry where Hedvig regularly stored food and cooking ingredients. The front room, with a large round oak table in front of the window facing the driveway, was the focal point of the house. People gathered there for all occasions: visiting, listening to the radio, and worrying. The worrying was done mostly at night by Hedvig who would sit at the table, watching the headlights of cars on the main road and praying that one set would turn into the driveway, signaling the return of her "boys" from a night of carousing.

There was one main pump for all drinking, cooking and watering livestock at Ernie's place. It was situated in a prominent spot close to the barn. The continuous pumping up and down of the handle brought the water up and out the spout. The water was delicious, and the well never went dry, even in the driest summer.

The cool water made the well a good place to keep watermelons, butter, and the milk Sven had to store for the milk truck to pick up every day. Meat buried in sawdust was also stored in the well. Even though there was no refrigeration, Ernie said they never got sick *because Mom was so careful.*

Sven planted trees in the thirties—mostly spruce, Balm of Gilead, poplars and lilacs, but also a cedar tree by the toilet and two big ones east of the barn. Ernie mentions the well-used outdoor toilet in one of his letters, shocking Tom, whose house contained an indoor bathroom with standard toilet paper instead of old Sears and Roebuck catalogs.

Ernie's farm was as diversified as any other in the community. It produced a variety of crops, vegetables, and fruit and raised chickens, hogs, and cattle. Sven kept horses for work—wild horses right off the Western range that had to be broken by Ed and Ocky before they would even eat grain.

There was a division of labor on Ernie's farm. Ed and Ocky (mostly) worked in the fields while Ernie and Fat helped Sven with the milking, which had to be finished before they could have breakfast. They got up at 4:00 a.m., called the cows in, fastened the stanchions around the cows' necks, set their stools and milk pails on the floor under the udders, and tried not to get hit in the eye with the switching tails while they milked. They had to hang kerosene lamps in the barn so they could see individual cows. Ernie speaks longingly about his desire to press his head against a cow's warm belly again and how good Laling's breakfast tasted when the milking was finished.

A description of the place that Ernie loved wouldn't be complete without mention of the summer kitchen where Hedvig spent hours cooking over a wood stove so the house wouldn't get so hot. The well-traveled sidewalk from the house to the summer kitchen also led to a little stool by the side of the kitchen where Sven sat and cut up the vegetables which Hedvig cooked and canned.

Ernie liked to talk about his home to Tom who seemed to be as impressed with Ernie's description of his way of life as Ernie was of Tom's. *"Tom laughed when I told him how we would all take baths on Saturday night in a big washtub and how we had to make our butter yellow by pinching an orange pill and then mixing it. Sometimes we wouldn't get it mixed very good and you would scold us in Scandinavian remember that, Laling?"*

(Note: Ernie was talking about Oleo margarine which was used instead of butter sometimes.)

It was a picturesque and well-functioning homestead, this place that Ernie loved so much. The house was opened to anyone who needed a good meal or just wanted some company. People enjoyed getting together to talk about hunting, politics and local gossip. When the conversation turned to politics, people formed their opinions on the basis of what they heard, since there was no radio and the newspaper carried mostly local stories. But the inevitable misinformation didn't take away from the liveliness of the discussions which distracted them from their day-to-day problems.

Another distraction from their ordinary lives were the revival meetings set up in available areas near the church. Wooden folding chairs and benches were arranged in rows under a canvas that served as a tent. The preacher greeted the flock, prayed, and delivered a passionate sermon, followed by the churchgoers singing familiar hymns. Ernie's favorite was "Bringing in the Sheaves."

July 9, 1932
Dear Pop, Mom and brothers.

I suppose by the time you get these few lines I will be in the hospital taking treatments. I sure hope that after taking these treatments, I can go home. Of course, I suppose I will have to take home some pills for pain, because the treatments always work afterward. But, anyway I sure hope that I can go home. I wonder who is going to take me to the hospital. Aunty said that if someone would take care of the baby, then she would go. But I aint worrying because God will take it in his hands and it will turn out all right. After the treatments, it will be easy to take a ride home, because I will be in good shape, and there is always somebody going up there.

But I wonder if I am going home after the treatments? Or do I have to stay and take more. I may have to stay here all summer and take treatments but I don't mind, as long as I am going home sometime. The time will come when I can go home to all of you.

It is hard to tell if I have to stay longer than the twelve days. I may have to stay and I may go home. But like Ed says—Everything will turn out okay. I will try to be patient because I know patience will help. And, if I can keep thinking that God will help me, then I'm sure he will.

Well, how are things running on the dear old farm? How does Pop, Mom and all of you feel? I hope that you feel real good. I sure am glad that you guys want to write to me. I like to read the interesting letters you write. You're lucky to be at the best place in the world and I'm lucky to have you as brothers. I feel sorry for

Tom because no one writes to him. I don't think many people care about him and to me that's sad. A guy who's sick needs people to care about him and I sure have that.

I don't feel so awful bad now, but I will feel still better after I get through with the treatments.

I am always supplied with pills from the hosp. so I don't mind the pain I have from the results of the treatments.

The pain is mostly in the back, but sometimes it starts in the legs and pretty near all over. It's bad when it comes, but then its bound to be some pain because think of the treatments. Electric! I will feel much better after the treatments, but it's hard telling if I can go home. I sure will be glad when the day comes when I can go home. I am quite homesick now but I will try to hold out, because I know it is necessary. Have you had any more rain? I hope the crops turn out allright. I hear that the Oats and barley are doing fine, but the Flax and Wheat aint so hot. I hope we get a good stand of that also. Did the hay turn out allright? I hope you get plenty this year.

Do you hunt anymore Ocky? I suppose there's a lot of weeds now so it's quite hard to see the game. Do you take Fat with you? Do that when you can. I know he misses me quite a bit.

How are the horses? Is "Danny" still as fat as usual? I suppose Maud is quite gone now. I sure would like to see her again even if she is only a horse.

Well, there sure isn't much to write about. I think I know a lot to write, but when it comes to writing I don't have nothing to say. It's funny how them things work in life when you want to do something but you can't because of some reason. Like in writing. I want to write because it makes me feel closer to you and the farm. But how much can I say when I don't do much. I feel so sorry for Tom. He hasn't seen his mother since he left home and started riding trains. I think about that a lot. It must have been some kind of life for all those kids, I'm glad I didn't have to do it.

I hope you will write soon again because theres nothing better I like to do than to read Ed's and Ocky's and Fat's letters. I sure like to read interesting letters, because I have nothing else to do. I will close with much love to all.

From Ernie. Please write soon. Don't worry dear "Laling" and don't worry the rest of you. Give my love to little Roy.

P.S. Have you guys heard of Mulligan Stew? Its what hobos eat, anything goes into a pot that they cook over a campfire, all kinds of vegetables whatever the hobos had in their pockets. Anyone who stops at a hobo camp can eat the stew and drink coffee from tin cups. Tom says that it's the life next to Chicago. He says the hobos have quite a time together, they sit around the campfire and tell stories and drink a little beer sometimes. It sure makes me lonesome for the farm, not the beer but being together like my Mom, Pop and Brothers.

Hobos gathered in places they called "jungles" to cook and wash, do laundry, or just rest. If one were to visit a shady jungle on the banks of a creek not far from the train yards, he/she would most likely find a variety of clothing drying on a willow tree, a cool stream for bathing—even a mirror planted in the trees for sharing. The basic possessions of a hobo were a razor, bar of soap, small towel, jack knife, pair of socks, and a collapsible aluminum drinking cup. Hobos encountered a number of sanitation and personal hygiene problems while being on the road. Among them was a shortage of restrooms, which had negative consequences. They learned never to go into a strange hobo camp after dark looking for a place to sleep for they were almost certain to lie down in something unpleasant. On a more positive note, a visitor would most definitely find a Mulligan Stew and coffee, waiting to be shared with anyone who stopped by.

Some jungles were nothing more than a clearing for a campfire, while others were well-established and run by old hobos who called the sites their homes. In either setting, one would likely find entire families, including children, who were not bums but people out of work and trying to get by. Some of the larger jungles served up to 100-150 people.

Except for the jungles where hobos felt secure and welcomed, they had to worry about safety and self-preservation, so they devised a method of communication among themselves, which non-hobos couldn't figure out. They would enter from the alley and knock on the back door of a house, hoping to be offered a good meal or a job. If this happened, they would return to the alley, but not before removing a piece of chalk from their pockets and drawing signs and symbols on fences or garage doors to alert other hobos.

They drew marks where the sick could go for aid, the starving for a free meal, and the thirsty for clean water supplies. They also marked where there were safe camps, dangerous towns and biting dogs.[12]

July 16, 1932
Dear Pop, Mom and brothers,

I have nothing to do today so I am writing in order to kill time. I can tell you I am getting homesick now. The more I think about home the more I want to see it. That's all I think of is home, sweet home.

At least I can see Tom again now that I'm back in the hospital. He's not doing to good. He talked about home a lot today. I wish someone would write to him, he's as lonesome as I am. I think I help him when I talk about the farm and he helps me when he talks about Chicago and his adventures.

When I have nothing else to do, I lay and look out of the window of the hospital and occasionally I see a cottontail rabbit hop across the opening. That brings back memories of hunting with all you guys, especially you Fat. I think about all the times we was in the woods we hunted anything we saw. And I think about the times we cleared the grove of rabbits that sure was fun. Tom and other hobos shot rabbits in the fields when they was hitchhiking. They roasted them over a fire. Guess they tasted pretty good, makes me wonder why we never ate rabbits. My brothers are good to me so when I think of dear Pop and Mom and brothers, tears start in my eyes. Yes sir, if any living person is homesick I am the one.

But don't let this worry you, because the day will come, when I too, can see my dear home land and all of you. It requires a great deal of patience, that's all.

I hope all of you feel real good. As for myself, I feel quite well and what's more, the gland in my leg and stomach are withering away. The Dr. said so also. My Dr. is a she. Her name is Dr. Day. I have another doctor besides that. To tell the truth there is nothing left except the pain, and that's so small that it's hardly worth counting on. But nevertheless it's hard telling if I may go home in 12 days. As for myself, I don't think I'll have to wait so awful long. Miss Eaves said 12 days or 2 weeks, but its hard telling. I know that when I do get out I'll have to take it mighty easy. I'll be nothing but skin and bones, white as a sheet, and weak as a mouse, so that I'll resemble a living skeleton more than anything else. I'm still tan but when I am in the hosp. a while that will soon go off.

How do things stand up there now? The crops ought to be good this year because its been warm and plenty of rain, here anyway. At least I hope they turn out good.

I bet the pasture is nice now, and that reminds me about "pot belly" Danny. Is he as fat as usual? I bet he's fatter than usual. How many cows is there now? Are they all milking good? I hope they can milk good in the wintertime in order to get a good cream check, but I suppose there aint much of a price on that either.

I wished I could be up there and help you pick blueberries, because I suppose they are ripe by now.

> *There'll be many pickers this year because of the new road. That was a handy shortcut. And saves many gallons of gas. I wonder if there are any blueberries in Hansons pasture this year. It was a good place last year but there were to many people there. I'd give anything if I could be up there in time for the picking, but I suppose I won't be that lucky. I wish you would write often because I get so awful homesick I don't know what to do. I love the farm with all my heart. The letters give me an idea of whats happening up there. I sure enjoy to read you guys letters, write soon will you Ed and Ock and Fat? I just received a letter from you and I was overjoyed to get it. Well, a shriveled up squirt like me will soon be sixteen years old. It seems impossible but it's true.*
>
> *Well, I sure haven't much to write about, but I'll say one thing more before I close and that is, that I'm longing for some good "Laling made" soup and good "Laling made" bread. I wish Tom could have that good food to. Do you know that.*
>
> *How do you feel lately, dear little "Laling?" And how are you Pop? I hope all of you feel real good. I will close with much Love to you all. From Ernie. Goodbye for the time being. Greet Little Roy and Fat and all of you from me, Ed please write real soon.*

(Note: There is no mention of any birthday celebration for Ernie.)

Tom told Ernie that things were good at home before the trouble started. His Dad had a steady job as a fireman in Chicago. He was a loving father with five children; Tom was the oldest. When his Dad lost his job and couldn't find another, everyone in the family found some way of making a contribution. One brother shined shoes in a barber shop; another delivered newspapers. His sister babysat and his mother sewed clothes and styled hair for people. But then those jobs fell apart because people could no longer afford to get their shoes shined or their hair done. They had no material for new clothes. Tom quit school but his sister and brothers kept going because it was warm in school. He struck out for California, having been told there were jobs there and life was better. His mother didn't want him to go and cried when he left, but his father encouraged him.

Before things got really bad at their house, Tom and his siblings would go to a movie once in a while. For ten cents, he told Ernie, a kid could see a double feature, a cartoon, news dealing with current events, a funny short story, and the latest chapter of an adventure story. When Tom told Ernie that the theater sometimes offered free ice cream, Ernie, who had never been to a movie, was dubious (.... *he couldn't of told the truth.*) As fascinated as he was by Tom's description of the theater, Ernie was even more impressed by the radio shows Tom said that he used to listen to, such as *The Lone Ranger, The Shadow* (*real spooky*) and *Will Rogers* (*real funny*). He also heard about comedians such as Amos and Andy and Fibber McGee. Ernie wished for a radio while he was in the hospital. It certainly would have made the time go faster for him.

July 19, 1932

(Note: Ernie's return address: E. Pearson; University Hospital; M2; Minneapolis, Minnesota)

Dear Pop, Mom and brothers.

I am writing a few lines in order to while away time. I am, as usual, feeling good outside of a few pains. I take pills to relieve it, but I could easily be without them, because the pains are not severe. But the Dr. said that they would do me no harm so therefore I take them. Outside of that I am fine. How are you feeling? I hope you are all in excellent shape, and I believe you are. Well, the time is soon here when I will go home. The Dr. told Aunty that I could probably go on Saturday or Sunday! This coming Sat. or Sun. Oh Boy!

Just think of it. I will soon be home to see you all. Of course, I must go back and take more treatments but anyway it will be a change. The Dr. didn't exactly know when I should be back but she would let us know. I never heard better news in my life. I can't wait to see the farm!

Them treatments do wonders. I'll tell you something. A young man, who had been bothered 4 years with the very same sickness as I have, took 11 treatments which entirely cured him. He stayed 2 months in the hospital and during that time he suffered awful with pain in the back. The other day I met him and he was all well. So you see! If I be patient and keep on taking treatments why, then, probably by the time I take 11 or 12 treatments, I will also be cured.

I hope the pain leaves me while I am home, but if it don't I can get pills to relieve it. All there is left is pain. The lumps on my leg is all gone and the place where the tumor was removed is all healed. I sure am glad that I can see the farm again. I am overjoyed! Once more I can take a little hunting trip. Of course, I shall have to take it easy.

To Fat: Here's my idea, Fat! I have 1 dollar and 6 cents. With it we will try to get a fairly good knapsack and some shells for our guns. Then, Dear brother Fat, you and I shall hit the trail together. Not so awful far, but I mean load our pack with "flesk," bread, eggs, salt, and some coffee. Oh Boy! Fat we'll have some fun. We'll take guns and shells. Goodbye for this time, Brother. From Ernie.

To Ed: Well, Ed, how are you coming along? I hope you are feeling good. Remember Ed you always used to say that there was something wrong with you? Well, I'll guarantee I never ran across better specimans than you or Ocky. What are you doing with yourself nowadays Ed? I bet you and Ocky are teasing each other about that Ines damsel. Ha, ha.

Have you been hunting lately? I suppose you all been working like dogs to get the hay up. I sure am glad to hear that there is enough of it. Take it easy Ed and don't overwork yourself. And the rest of you take it easy too. Well, I will see you again and I sure am glad.

By the way I've had 4 treatments already. Two more to go. Love to all from Ernie.

To Ocky: How are you Ock? I hope you are o.k. I hear you got 2 slashers this year, so far. Well, that sure was good. I hear from you that you got the tent back. I sure am glad because that was a nifty little tent. Well, I will soon see you again Ock. So goodbye, with much love to you all from Ernie. Goodby Little Laling and Pop and Roy.

Hodgkin lymphoma was, and still is, an insidious disease. It's been compared to shooting at a moving target and, unlike most other cancers, cannot be cut from the body. The radiation zaps one affected area and the patient feels good until the cancer moves to another part of the body. In 1932, without the combination chemotherapy and radiation treatment available today, the disease ultimately got so far ahead of the treatment that there was no chance of catching up.

Ernie sustained a positive attitude throughout, even when he knew deep down, there was a possibility that he wouldn't get well. He never gave up because he was so full of life and wanted desperately to enjoy his family and the farm again. He was equally concerned about his parents and brothers and kept encouraging them to remain positive and not worry. Toward the end, however, he expressed a belief that it might not be God's will that he get well; other plans were being made for him over which he had no control.

July 21, 1932
Dear Pop, Mom and Brothers.

This won't be a very long letter because I will soon be seeing you. I'm so glad I don't know what to do. I sit for hours and think of our dear little farm, and I sure got an appetite for the things "Laling" cooks, especially the home- made bread. To tell the truth I am so sick of city bread that I don't care whether I get it or not. In the hospital I haven't seen the sign of an egg, but wait till I get home. And "Flesk"! Oh Boy! Yes, I sure am hungering for the things on the farm. Its more healthier, better and more nourishing eats than what you get in the city. But wait till I get home. I think I can get out Sat. because my treatments will be completed on Friday. I'm taking the last one tomorrow. It too will be done by the time you get this letter.

I asked the Dr. if I could get up and go out in the sun, and he said I could. I am much better now, after I've taken the treatments. Like I said, all there's left now is the little pain I have in the back. But that's so small that its hardly worth mentioning. I can get some pills from the Dr, in case I need them. But anyway it will be the greatest pleasure to get home for a while. Of course, I got to take it awful easy. Just walk around the yard a little, that's all. As soon as I feel myself tired I must go and lay down. I haven't asked the Dr. when I should come back for more treatments, but I suppose it will be in a month or so.

Tom is pretty sick now. All he can do is lay in bed. But he still talks. One thing I can say about Tom's stories is they always take my mind off the farm and my Mom, Pop and bros. for a little while. Today he talked about them hobos again. He said that he sometimes slept in places called "jungles" that was for hobos. He washed his clothes there and sometimes they had mirrors planted in the trees for sharing with anyone who needed to shave. Aint that great? Once he almost got killed though because some hobo wanted his shoes. That's where they ate that Mulligan Stew I told you about.

How are things coming up there? Have you had any rain lately? We just had a shower last night but it didn't amount to much.

Are the cattle and horses in good shape? I sure hope they are. And I am glad to hear that my little calf is coming along good. I bet he'll be fat and nice by fall. I forgot whether it was a bull or heifer but I think it's a heifer. How many baby turkeys is there? Fat wrote and told me once but I forgot. I suppose Harold will come with us up there.

I sure am pale now. I'm as white as a sheet and I'm as skinny as can be, but I'll soon pick up. And I forgot to tell you that I got a mighty good appetite. How are all you feeling now? I hope you're all well. I will close with much love to you all. From Ernie. I received your letters and sure was glad to get them.

It has been said that the sense of smell is our most potent memory trigger but, for Ernie, it was a deep, painful longing for a world he used to know that made him remember. It was this longing that penetrated his letters and turned them into bittersweet, nostalgic stories and poignant reminiscences, written solely to and for his concerned family living on his beloved farm.

In one of his letters, Ernie was comforting Tom whose house—the place he'd grown up in—had to be sold and his family separated. He said, *I told Tom that it ain't important that his house is gone. When he leaves here, he can go back to his Mom and Pop and that will be his home. But Tom kept talking about all the things he wished he would of done for his mother.*

This part of the book cannot have a happy ending. Ernie's last letter was written on July 21st. We know that Ernie died in August at the farm, so this part of his wish came true. What we don't know is how much time he had to spend with his parents, brothers, and animals. We don't know whether his pain was managed through medication well enough to allow him to participate in any farm activities. Did he have one last hunting trip with Fat? Probably not; he would have been too weak to trample in the woods he loved. But, he most certainly basked in the love of his family who, according to Fat, were comforted by Ernie's last words: *I'll see you all in Heaven.*

About Tom, we only know from Ernie's last letter that he was very sick. There is more reason to believe that he died in the hospital after Ernie went home than to believe that he recovered and joined his family, wherever they were. Did he die alone, or was his mother with him at the end? I hope that the latter is true, because the alternative—dying alone—is too horrible to affix to the memory of a gregarious, sweet fifteen-year-old boy.

Two young men—boys, really—were bedfellows in a sad place during a horrible period about which an unsophisticated farm boy and a pseudo- worldly city boy understood little. While their upbringings and experiences were vastly different, they found solace in each other's company. Their illness, homesickness, and loneliness should have crushed their spirits, but it was not to be. One is led to believe that their indomitable spirits triumphed until the end.

It would not be unreasonable for the reader to be wondering, at this point, how a transition from a 1932 Great Depression story to World War II remembrances will be made in the second part of this book. The connection is Fat who, thirteen years after Ernie's death, still thought about his brother and lamented his loss.

Part Two

Raymond

It was hard to understand just how much poverty there was across America— even after the war. Working class families lived from day to day, just as they had been doing since the beginning of the thirties, especially in rural America. Ernie and Raymond, their family, and everyone they knew were poor, and yet their worlds were filled with possibility and hope.

Ernie was just a carefree shirt-tailed kid before he became sick, and Fat a father and lumberjack before he was drafted. Neither one allowed some large outside force, i.e., illness or the war, to define him. Their lives were defined by their passions, not by what was happening to them. They both had a clear, simple dream of returning to the place they loved most and to an anxious mother who hoped for the best and prayed that God would bring her sons home. And "home" was the farm in Falun,

Minnesota, which stood for simple goodness and a lack of ambivalence—a place where people understood one another, where hard work and love of family mattered a lot.

April, 1945-January, 1946
December 7, 1941 Extra!
Japs Declare War on U.S. Planes Bomb Pearl Harbor, Manila Bombs Set U.S. Battleships Afire
350 Killed
(Headlines in the *St. Paul Pioneer Press*)

It was a typical Sunday morning at the U.S. Naval base in Hawaii on December 7, 1941. Pearl Harbor was a picture of serenity with 145 vessels of all kinds, from small boats to big battleships, resting peacefully in the harbor. Suddenly, 200 Japanese fighter planes attacked at 7:55 and then again at 8:30, damaging or destroying 19 warships, including eight battleships, and killing more than 2400 U.S. soldiers and sailors. The battleships—Oklahoma, Arizona, California, West Virginia, Tennessee, Nevada, Pennsylvania, and Maryland—were hit in the first few minutes. Most sank immediately or as a result of heavy damage. It wasn't long before the once-peaceful harbor became a place of destruction.

After destroying the harbor, the Japanese attacked the airfield where planes had been lined up in the center of the field in a deliberate attempt to prevent a sneak attack. As it turned out, this configuration made it easy for the attacking planes which destroyed 188 U.S. aircraft. If the US Navy's aircraft carriers had not been out on maneuvers, however, the destruction would have been even worse.

Did the Americans have any warning that they were about to be attacked? How had the United States been caught so completely off guard? There were actually two occurring events that could have been considered warnings. The Americans sank a Japanese submarine near the entrance to the harbor but didn't realize that it was the precursor to a large attacking force. Also, at 7 o'clock that morning, an Army radar installation detected a large formation of planes approaching the harbor but dismissed it as an unofficial training exercise by U.S. B-17 bombers flying in from California. Either one of these events might have provided enough notice to disperse aircraft and fly off reconnaissance if it had been taken seriously.

Why did the Japanese attack Pearl Harbor? Japan and America were not traditional enemies, but tension between the two countries had been mounting for years. Finally, President Roosevelt imposed such severe conditions upon Japan, such as pressure to get out of China, that Japan was forced to strike. While Roosevelt wanted Japan to strike the first blow, he didn't expect it to be as devastating as Pearl Harbor, and he didn't have have any guarantee that an attack by Japan would result in a U.S. declaration of war against Germany (which was the war that Roosevelt really wanted to get into because he was worried that the Allies couldn't win without the U.S.) In fact, what happened was predictable: Even when America responded with a declaration of war against Germany after Pearl Harbor, people couldn't understand why we just didn't go to war with Japan.

There was also the desire of Japan to be the dominant power in East Asia, but the U.S., with its presence in the Philippines, was a major stumbling block. From all accounts, the Pearl Harbor attack was necessary for Japan to survive, for it to fulfill its "manifest destiny," which was to subjugate and dominate all of the other Asian countries they believed to be inferior. Feeling threatened by the U.S. and its potential for stopping her conquests, Japan had to destroy the American force.

Admiral Yamamoto, commander of the Japanese fleet, didn't want a war, but he was told to stop the Pacific Fleet and decided that an attack on Pearl Harbor would do it. He recognized that in a long, drawn-out war, Japan couldn't win, but if the U.S. Navy could be crippled quickly, by the time it was rebuilt and the U.S. came back, Japan would be in control. He mistakenly thought that the United States was too soft and weak to pursue a war. Yamamoto and his country couldn't have been more wrong in underestimating the resilience of the U.S. and its willingness to go to war.

On December 7th, President Roosevelt announced in a Honolulu newspaper that the Japanese had attacked Pearl Harbor in a daring military operation that had the advantages of a total surprise and a target that was completely unprepared. He called December 7th "a date which will live in infamy". On December 11, Germany and Italy declared war on the United States, and the U.S. answered with its own declaration of war on Germany and Italy. World War II became global and America a full participant. The world's strongest navy, Germany, was aligned with the world's strongest army, Japan. Both countries became enemies with the greatest war-making potential in the world, the United States.[13]

The Japanese were so confident about Admiral Yamamoto's indestructibility in his superiority over the Americans after Pearl Harbor that, within hours of the attack, they continued to capture islands throughout the Western Pacific and attacked American positions in the Philippines. The United States was devastated, especially by its dramatic defeat in the Philippines where MacArthur had to flee, leaving his troops trapped on Corregidor and forced to march 65 miles through the jungle in lacerating heat with little food and water. Survivors of the Bataan Death March became slave laborers in Japan.

Then the U.S. began to recover its equilibrium, and MacArthur organized an island-hopping campaign toward Japan. He gave the Japanese their first defeat with the Battle of the Coral Sea followed by another with the Battle of Midway.

In June, 1942, Japan made the decision to sail for Midway to teach the Americans a lesson by annihilating their fleet. Their goal was to try for a surprise attack like Pearl Harbor, and they counted on taking the island in one massive stroke. The Americans, however, had anticipated the attack and, unlike Pearl Harbor, were prepared. Admirals Nimitz and Spruance together made several wise decisions on Midway that resulted in a remarkable victory for the United States and demoralized Japan, who suffered an unrecoverable loss of aircraft carriers. Historians claim that Midway was one of the most decisive battles in the history of the world. It changed the course of World War II.

Two months later, the Americans scored another victory which also helped turn the tide of the Pacific War. Guadalcanal was an island where the Japanese were building an airfield that they planned to use for launching planes in order to fly further with heavier bombs. U.S. forces took the airfield with little difficulty, but the Japanese swiftly retaliated by sinking four heavy American cruisers. What saved the United States was Japan's premature departure, which gave the Americans time to win the battle. The Battle of Guadalcanal is considered to be the first major U.S. assault in the Pacific War.[14]

When we talk about World War II we wrongly think of only one war. In reality, the war in the Pacific and the war in Europe made "The Great War" two wars, which were distinct and fought simultaneously. Against Japan, America fought alone, and the Pacific Theater would be mostly America's war. In Europe, however, America was part of an Allied Force.

In the European Theater, World War II was considered by many to be an extension of World War I in that Hitler set out to reverse all of the restrictions he believed the Treaty of Versailles had imposed unfairly on Germany. Once considered to be the soul of Germany, Hitler violated the arms limitations clauses of the Treaty of Versailles by rebuilding the German army, navy, and air force. He forced both Austria and Czechoslovakia to become part of Germany. In 1939, he invaded Poland, despite Britain's insistence that Poland would be protected against German aggression. When Poland fell, Great Britain and France declared war on Germany, starting the Second World War in Europe.

During this time, the United States, Britain and France were still dealing with the Great Depression, which was having an enormous impact throughout Europe, especially on Germany because the government was dependent upon American finance. While the U.S. was working to rebuild its battered economy, Hitler was winning overwhelming support from the German people for his Nazi party. Everyone knew what Hitler was doing but the Allies didn't try to stop him, probably because they were all busy attending to their own problems. President Roosevelt felt that the war was an essentially European affair and didn't want to become involved militarily. It was a pivotal moment when Roosevelt passed the Lend Lease Act in 1941, enabling him to give military equipment to England and Russia, thereby allowing the United States to fight the war without getting Americans killed. When

Germany declared war on the United States, however, America could no longer remain isolated and neutral in Europe.

It was the worst war ever fought. We were slow in getting in and we endured a lot of tragedy, but we had a better war than the Europeans and Russians had (quote from one of Raymond's last letters written during the reconstruction of Germany). History would seem to validate this observation: For years, Russian, English, and French troops would do most of the fighting and take the brunt of the beating. And it would be Stalin's troops who would really beat Hitler.

In terms of the numbers, the territory, and the damage done to Germany, the Russian contribution was indispensable. More than 20 million Russians died. It was likely that for every American who perished in World War Two, 50 Russians lost their lives. Looking at it another way, the number of Americans who died on the first day of the Normandy invasion was fewer than half the average Russian loss every day of the war, most as a result of combat with the Germans.[15]

Camp Maxey, Texas
(April 15-August 12, 1945)

Thirteen years after Ernie wrote letters home to Sven and Hedvig and his brothers, Raymond was drafted into the Army and repeated the practice. His letters are replete with references to Ernie whose memory was still very much alive. Because the bond between Ernie and Raymond was so strong while

Ernie was alive and still felt after he had died, I wanted the reader to have a feeling for who Raymond was as a young man and, similarly, who Ernie probably could have been if he had lived—according to his brother and best friend, Fat.

Raymond was eighteen when he married Myrtle in 1937. They had no money at the time so they, along with their baby daughter, Jean, lived with Myrtle's widowed mother and Raymond's parents until they were able to buy eighty acres of land from the government. They built a little house, and Raymond farmed his land and worked as a lumberjack in the winter until he got drafted on April 12, 1945, the day that the man who had steadfastly guided Americans through four years of the war collapsed and died. President Roosevelt's sudden death affected Raymond. He wrote that *"it was a sad day for our country and for me, since I really didn't want to go."*

Now it was April 15, 1945. Raymond was twenty-seven years old and in the Army, separated from Myrtle and Jean. For more than eighteen months, most of his communication was the V-mail letter, flimsy sheets of paper that were often inadequate for him to be able to write all that he wanted to say. There were long strings of empty days without letters, and Raymond complained about those dry spells. It was especially frustrating for him not to receive letters when those he wrote were lengthy descriptions of news about him and the world around him. In some way, he felt responsible for writing letters to not only his immediate family but to people in his extended family, including aunts and uncles in Norway. He wrote prolifically because he knew that the only way to receive letters was to write them.

In his letter from Camp Maxey, Texas, he describes his eighteen-hour train ride from St. Paul, Minnesota as an ordeal that included orders for the soldiers not to leave the car they were assigned to and only two meals that *were mighty poor, so you can imagine how a guy with my appetite felt.* He was happy to finally arrive at Camp Maxey where, for the first few days, it had been one endless round of red tape—insurance classification, long lectures on military courtesy, detailed instructions on how to salute an officer, and hundreds of other *tiresome things.* It was the day the soldiers were fitted for their uniforms that Raymond was hit by the reality that he belonged to Uncle Sam. He also became acutely aware of his appearance in uniform: *When I got out of the clothing issue and went over to the barracks and looked at myself in the mirror, I couldn't help but be proud of my looks. I sure am a husky soldier if I must say so myself. When you look at all the puny little runts, skinny guys, huge fat men, you see some odd sights. A man can be proud of the build he has got.*

Struck by the stark difference between army and civilian life, Raymond describes a typical day in the Army after he had been in camp for less than two week. *Today we stood in the hot sun for four hours and drilled, and drilled, and drilled some more. After that we had chow and then we were marched about four miles to another section of the army. There they gave us shots in the right and left arms for lockjaw and smallpox. The docs just jammed the needle in full hilt and didn't really care that it hurt. After that we were marched back again to stand retreat. That means we stand stiff and straight in four perfect lines at attention. The bugler played Taps. An officer came out and it was "face front, right face, dress company" and all sorts of commands that lasted 30 minutes. I've never been given so many orders in so little time before. I thought for sure we were done for the day but we still had to work on our rifles and polish them for an hour and a half. We were finally allowed to go for chow. After wolfing down some grub we were ordered back to the barracks to prepare for clothing inspection. We had to lay all our clothes and equipment in neat rows on our bunks and then we had to stand there for almost an hour while two officers checked them over. After that, we were allowed to do as we pleased until 9:00 when it's lights out in the barracks. Believe me, 9:00 couldn't come soon enough for me and no one argued about going to sleep that early.*

The difference between army life and civilian life couldn't have been made clearer than it was on the day Raymond discovered that his bunk was short a pillow. He mustered all of his courage to ask the Master Sergeant if he could get another one. The terse reply was, "Don't bother me, Fellow. Go to the Supply Sergeant." Raymond did just that, only to be told to beat it once again. He ended up repeating his request to two more officers and receiving the same response. Feeling pretty sure that he was going to have to adjust to sleeping with one thin pillow, he was surprised to find two pillows on his bunk when he returned to the barracks that evening. *I guess you just have to get used to being kicked around in the army.*

One of the recurring themes in Raymond's letters was the conflict he felt about his commitment to God at this point in his life. Having grown up in a solid Christian home with parents who spoke as much about the future when they would be in Heaven as they did about the present when they were still a part of life here on earth, Raymond believed that he too should focus on Eternity. The problem arose when earthly pleasures tempted him to do things that he felt pretty sure would prevent him from going to Heaven. More than once, he succumbed to the temptations, largely because they were so prevalent in the Army. Army life was a shocking eye-opener for Raymond. There were so many sins.

When I look around the barracks there's poker games in progress, cursing, dice rolling and a lot of guys are out in the canteen bailing down beer. I just can't figure guys out. In a few months they'll be facing death and there isn't one thought to Eternity. That's one thing I thank my God for that I can pray to him at night and ask his help to guide and protect me through this battle that's ahead. When I was in Fort Sumpter I went to the canteen and to the bar and bought beer. After I had drunk a few bottles I started thinking and it wasn't long before I was back in the barracks asking God's forgiveness. And he forgave me too because pretty soon that old peace was back in my heart that I felt when I was first saved. Then I realized that I had something that all the things in the world can't take the place of and it sure is a blessed assurance to have. When I left home I had the thought in my mind that I was going to have my fun too. But the kind of reckless life I lived before I was drafted can never go for me anymore.

As time went on and Raymond became more jaded about army life, it seemed that he was able to relax a little, but there was always the fear of facing death with a soul that wasn't right with God. He felt he had to keep trying to be good enough for God, and when he failed in that endeavor (as he was bound to do), he despaired at his weakness. While he was merciless in his self-condemnation, however, he stopped short of condemning others who engaged in what he perceived as wrongdoings against God. Indeed, he was more perplexed than judgmental: How could men sin so freely without giving any thought to the severe consequences of their sin, especially when the possibility of dying was very real?

Lester Mitterling was from Raymond's home town of Roseau, Minnesota. He belonged to the 103rd Battalion which was only five blocks from where Raymond was housed, and Raymond was glad to have a Christian buddy, even though they didn't see each other very often. Raymond thought that Lester was the only guy around who didn't make fun of Christianity and believed as he did: There are no atheists in a foxhole, and many of the same men who scorned God on a daily basis would be praying for His mercy when they found themselves on the battlefield. Lester and Raymond went to tent meetings that were held in a nearby town, but they were always disappointed in the preachers who spent more time and energy asking for money than they did preaching the Gospel. The night that the evangelist badgered the people into meeting his goal of $150 marked the end of tent meetings and the beginning of the pair's attendance at the Bible Baptist Church, which they found to be much more to their liking, at least for a time.

Raymond was very concerned about the spiritual status of his brothers, Roy and Ocky, and wrote about how he needed to know that their hearts were right with God, so he would have a heavenly future with them if anything happened to him while he was in the Army. About his brother Ed, however, he had no doubts. Ed's faith was solid like his parents, as was Ernie's before he died. *It's funny how I've been thinking a lot about Ernie since I got here. He probably would have been here with me. He loved to fight and he was good at it too. I remember you told me what Dr. Berge said, Pa, that if anyone could beat that disease, it would be Ernie. Well, God didn't see it that way even though we all prayed hard for his healing.*

He summed up his family's spiritual state (*This is the way I see it....*) by acknowledging that if he were to die while in the Army, he would most certainly see his mother and father in Heaven, along with Ed and Ernie, and his wife and daughter. He wasn't so sure about Roy and Ocky.

At least for the first couple of months, Raymond found the Army to be inhospitable to Christianity. As things stood, he felt that trying to live a Christian life in the Army was a losing battle. *I try to be true to God but I have no one to talk to about him. If only I had someplace to go where I could be with some real Christians it would be a lot easier. But one thing I thank God for is that he won't let me go.... When I wrote to you a few days ago that I had peace in my soul again I was pretty happy. But then I was tempted so terrific and I thought to myself what's the use, I can never be what God wants me to be anyway. So I weakened again. But I can't face what I'm going through without knowing that I am truly saved. So I'm never going to give up....*

At one level Raymond lived the Gospel, the good news of Jesus Christ, but then he would return to the man-made rules of religion and a faith based on works instead of grace. It escaped his attention that repentance for one's motivations for his right-doings is just as important—maybe even more so— as repentance for his wrongdoings. The good works faith got him into trouble every time. Rather than believing in a God who was watching him at every moment, ready to catch him if he happened to do something wrong, Raymond might have been happier focusing his attention on the loving God who delights in his creation and wants his people to do the same.

Because he was so afraid of not being good, Raymond was unable to derive much enjoyment out of army life, at least in the beginning. He never considered the possibility that not all army extra-curricular activities, e.g., line dances and beauty contests, were immoral. He could have joined in the fun without feeling guilty and, if he had done so, he would have been a lot less bored on Saturday nights.

Gradually, Raymond became fatalistic about his future, believing that there was nothing he could do to alter it. The only thing that he felt was in his control was his faith, his belief that if he did go to battle and was killed, he knew where he was headed. That was his armor. The months that he spent in training and post-war overseas reconstruction undoubtedly gave him a personal focus and an understanding of what was important in his life: his faith, his family, hard work, and the small part of America that he loved.

Raymond was aware of the lack of mental intimacy in a war. The men in his battalion lived close to each other and they talked about many things. But, since everyone was in the same perilous situation, no one could give any real consolation, so Raymond turned to God, which to him seemed to be the natural thing to do. Besides, he met men on a weekly basis who had touched death and danger, and they called on God when they were in tough spots.

In his loneliest times, Raymond said that home felt different for him. It was the smallest, most trivial details about home—those that he took for granted during normal times—that he missed most of all. *It's a funny thing when a guy gets far from home. He takes more interest in things at home than he ever did.*

While Raymond's life was definitely anchored in the world of real values, he engaged in some theorizing and high-blown sentiments from time to time. For example, after an especially trying day of deferring to commanding officers and standing at rigid attention until a general had found his particular place in a room, Raymond posited that if people paid half as much attention to God as they do to generals, flag, and country, the world would be a different (and better) place. He amended his opinion by then suggesting that in 1945, people associated God with generals, flag, and country and, if that were true, they were, indeed, paying Him a lot of attention.

A related topic on which Raymond expounded with mixed feelings was the role of the chaplain in the army. On the one hand, he had no use for chaplains because they were afraid to talk about God, preferring instead to refer to God in some general sense, i.e., our Maker. He believed that the chaplain was doing a disservice to the men by not preparing them for death. In believing that the chaplain performed no useful function, Raymond decided that he wouldn't attend chapel, that his time would be better spent reading his New Testament.

Another example of Raymond's distaste for army chaplains occurred when all of the Minnesota guys in his unit were told they were going to be riflemen in the same squad for training, that is, everyone except one of the Norstebon twins. The Army, in its infinite wisdom, split up Melvin and Alvin. Raymond was horrified. *They put me and one of the Norstebon twins and Adam Efta from Greenbush in the 1st Platoon 4th Squad so now we are all set to start training. But just think how dirty they are to split up the Norstebon twins. They even went to the Chaplain to get him to talk to the commanding officer but it didn't do any good. He wouldn't even listen. It sure is a shame they split up twin brothers that way. But I guess the army has no mercy for any man. If a man gets hard-boiled in here it's nothing to wonder at....*

In a couple of other letters Raymond shared a different opinion by referring to an army chaplain as the best friend a soldier could have, possessing solutions to most problems. The best example of this high praise is when he went to see the chaplain for advice on how to find a room in town for Myrtle whom he desperately wanted to see.

When I walked into his office and he was sitting there with captains bars on his shoulders, I felt pretty small because a captain is a pretty high officer in the army. So I saluted him but he brushed the salute aside and told me to sit down and make myself at home. In a few minutes of talking I felt like I had known him for many years. I asked him if he knew if there was any chance to rent a room in town for my wife. He said, "You're in luck soldier because I've been in town today and I spotted a nice room." So he called up the lady who's got the room and bragged me up so terrific and recommended me highly. She said that it would be okay as long as there wouldn't be any kids. If it wasn't for that chaplain I would never have been able to bring Myrtle here. He was a real compassionate man and humble too.

While he was in training, Raymond thought that army life was pretty tough. He suggested that staying in the army took all the guts a man possesses. From morning to night, it was one big rush with little time to rest or think. In one letter, he complained that they had to get up at 3:30 every morning in order to march four and a half miles, carrying a 40-pound field pack and their rifles, to get to the rifle range. *If that doesn't put a guy away, nothing will. I guess I didn't know what it meant to be tired until I got in the army.*

One morning, his company (which had been reduced to fewer than 100 men, down from the original 200—*they can't take infantry training so they're transferred to the Air Corps so that must be a pretty scabby outfit)* marched six miles to the rifle range with full field packs and stayed there all day firing the M1s. They thought they would be spending the night at the site, but at 8:00 orders came though the battalion headquarters that they had to march eight more miles before they could pitch their tents. At midnight they arrived at the bivouac area, pitched their tents and hit the sack only to get the order to fall out at 3:30. Raymond said that he rolled out of his blanket, feeling so groggy he could hardly see where he was going. They laid mines and booby traps all through the night. *Boy, was I played out. But I know now that I can take anything the Army can give me. And I know that I have to stay here so I might as well not kick about it. And if I want to be honest, I've never felt better in my life. Maybe it's not so bad being a Doughboy....*

In another letter, he mentioned that they had just returned from a 14-mile jaunt that made him feel a little faint. But that was nothing compared to what they had to do the next day when they left camp at 5:00 a.m. and marched for two hours and then spent all day practicing combat formation—with only one canteen of water, which didn't last long in the Texas heat. *And it's starting to take a toll on me too. You know I weighed 220 pounds when I left home. Well, now I have gone down to 190 pounds so I've lost 30 pounds. It's the heat I can't stand. When we are on a march we can ring the sweat out of our fatigue jackets. And they say this is nothing compared to July and August. I can't see how I'm going to make it then.*

Raymond's worst weather fears were confirmed: The heat situation did get worse in July. While his family was celebrating the Fourth of July in Falun, Minnesota, Raymond's unit got up at 3:30, ate breakfast, and headed out for the light machine gun range. In spite of the searing temperatures, Raymond was looking forward to the event. He thought it would be a lot of fun, firing 250 rounds in one minute. But the heat was too much, even for the gun. It didn't stop firing when Raymond released the trigger. The heat of the red hot barrel kept the cartridges going off, and the rest of the unit just stood there watching Raymond fire away. Feeling hot and foolish, he wished that he were anywhere but where he was—preferably back on the farm where it was a lot cooler and he was with his family.

A sense of humor shows through in many of Raymond's letters. In one letter, he described the course the Army was giving them in hand-to-hand combat and was particularly impressed with all the "tricks" they were being taught to subdue the enemy with bare hands. In one of his classes, the instructor picked Raymond to demonstrate some moves. *Before I knew what was happening, he grabbed my hand, made a twist, and threw me over his shoulder and I landed hard on the ground. I picked myself up and looked him straight in the eye and told him to get some other greenhorn to take advantage of. After I've had some training in this kind of warfare, I hope that runty corporal asks for a volunteer again, so I can break his neck.*

There was also the demonstration that Major Slater, who commanded the 108th Battalion, gave on shooting from the hip. Raymond said that the Major was rated as one of the best hip shooters in the U.S. Army. *First, he took a 45 and fired from the hip. Then he took a carbine in each hand and poured lead into the targets at 50 yards. Then he took a 30 Caliber Machine Gun and fired a whole cartridge belt from the hip. I've never seen such shooting in all my life. How he could hold that bucking machine gun at his hip and still hit the targets is a mystery to me. He sure must be a tough old hide. He also fired the M rifle. He put the butt of the rifle in his belly and slammed seven shots out of nine through a small target at 50 yards. I would hate to be a Japanese soldier and bump into that guy in the jungle. He wouldn't live two seconds. But then, I most likely wouldn't live very long either.*

Raymond seemed to enjoy taking little snipes at the Army. He was, at the same time, impressed with the demonstrations and bemused at the Army's efforts to make the soldiers do things the way they were trained... . *sure is fun to watch those guys out on the Machine Gun Range. They don't use sights or any of the methods the Army teaches us to use. The Crackmen who help in training handle the guns the way they did when they were in action, firing from the hip and sitting behind the gun when they should be in a prone position. It's really something to see the way they can spray those targets. They tell us when we get across we will be the same way. I guess a guy forgets all those gun positions you learn here and just do it you own way when you're in action.*

In a conversation with an old sergeant, Raymond asked him if he liked the Army. The sergeant replied in his Southern drawl, "Son, any man that likes the army just isn't normal. The days seem like weeks and the weeks are like months, right? There aint a man in the whole United States Army who wouldn't take a discharge if it was offered to him."

Mixed in with Raymond's conflicted view of the Army—mostly dislike at this point—was a measure of respect for the present military situation and the reality of war. The war in Europe was largely being fought by eighteen-year- old boys who possessed a sense of optimism that the war would end and they would be okay because they were so well trained. Raymond, being older, didn't share this sense of invincibility at all. He knew that people die in combat and training is no protection from reality. In fact, he believed that there was a good chance that he would be hurt or killed before the war was over. This is one of the times that his age and maturity made a difference... .

He worried about the optimism that prevailed among the troops because Germany was on the verge of defeat and the European conflict was drawing to a close. *The people who are in the know think just the opposite, that the future looks pretty black. And it sure is when you think that within 20 weeks you can be at the front. I see in the papers that the Germans are crumbling fast and that mess shouldn't last much longer. But if you ask me I think the Japanese are going to be hard to take. And that's what they tell us too. They don't try to smooth over the truth either. They tell us to train hard and do our utmost to learn all we can. Because when we get to the front and face an experienced enemy we'll need it. And that's no lie. When I look at some of these 18-year old kids that haven't even got beards on their faces yet, I could cry because it's such a shame they have to be here. They'll find out soon enough that war takes the cockiness out of you mighty fast and they won't be able to bullshit their way out the first time they're under fire.*

The "kids" he felt the most sorry for were the medics. Based upon reports from soldiers who had fought in battle, Raymond thought that the hardest job in the Army was that of a medic. Medics had to be extraordinarily brave and dutiful, since they administered simple treatment under the most difficult circumstances. One returning soldier told him about trench foot which became the scourge of foxholes. He said that his foxholes filled with water and then froze. Having no access to dry socks and boots, he had to have both feet amputated. Medics also had to deal with self-inflicted wounds which were common among frontline infantry when the going got tough. Then there was the fear that compelled men to dessert. Medics had to help these soldiers deal with their strong feelings. In many cases their religious convictions and beliefs helped them provide counseling.

While Raymond had mixed feelings about army chaplains, he possessed nothing but pure disdain for the doctors. *For once in my life, I wish I wasn't so healthy as I am. There are a lot of guys dropping out every day because they can't take it. I'm sorry to say I never felt better in my life.* Right after he uttered that wish, he had a headache that made him go on sick call. He asked the doctor for the day off until his headache got better. But the doctor laughed at him and said that a big bruiser like him shouldn't pay any attention to a little headache. So he was back on duty again. Later in the day, he strained a "cord" in his stomach when they were doing calisthenics. It hurt so much that he thought he had ruptured himself. The company commander told him to go to the doctor to find out what was wrong. It turned out to be only a bad strain, but Raymond could hardly walk, so he believed he should get the rest of the day off. But that was not to be. The doctor not only ordered him back on duty again, but Raymond had to go with the rest of the company on a five-mile march with full field equipment! Feeling wretched, but still looking good, he could only draw one conclusion: *When a guy looks fit, regardless of how he feels, the army has no mercy.*

There were so many soldiers who went on sick call to get out of a few hours of work that the battalion commander gave an order: Anyone who goes on sick call and is later found not to be sick enough to warrant the rest will lose all chances of a week-end pass. Since he wanted the weekend passes badly, Raymond was very careful about trying to go on sick call. It was too risky.

The one other time he had to go on sick call, the army doctors did little to alleviate whatever pain he was experiencing, which led Raymond to conclude that, not only were the army doctors merciless, but they were also incompetent.

I had a big molar pulled about a week ago and some kind of infection has set in my jawbone. It keeps aching night and day so I suppose I have to go and see these wonder doctors again and see if they can do something about it. But I suppose all they will do is give me some of those all-purpose pills that they give you for all the ailments a guy has. These army doctors are the most heartless and worthless guys I've ever known. Harry Stucy, a guy from Thief River Falls, is almost ready to keel over from a heart attack. But when he goes on sick call all they do is give him some AP pills and send him back to duty again. So it really isn't much use to go on sick call. It's going to be bad if Harry dies because of lack of medical attention. It will be too bad for the army.

Myrtle stayed around for a six-week period to be with Raymond as much as possible and then went home to Jean. While it was good to have her in town, Raymond felt bad when his unit went on bivouac for several days at a time, and he left Myrtle sitting in a sparsely furnished room waiting for him to show up for a few hours. Still, he missed her after she was gone, especially on Saturday nights when he had little to do other than think about when he would be going home. *The day I step off the train in Roseau will be the happiest day of my life.*

Raymond was a worrier. He had already established himself as a farmer and lumberjack in Northern Minnesota when he was drafted. Before he left, he entrusted his land to his brothers and counted on them to seed and harvest the crop. Even though he trusted them implicitly, and was verbally appreciative of their efforts, he voiced some apprehension about things that were being done in his absence, mostly because of lack of information.

He also worried about the little church in which he had grown up. Letters from home described how divided the congregation was over the question of moving the church to a more desirable location. Raymond was concerned that the debate and havoc would create a divisiveness from which the church would never recover. His concern turned out to be justified when Myrtle wrote that the final decision was to move the church and, as expected, this decision by the pastor was causing trouble among the members. While Raymond didn't agree with the pastor's decision, he exhorted his family to support it.... *Shragge* (pastor) *might have his faults but I think he is a real Christian and we have to stick by him.... we all have to be together in this if that church is going to bring any souls to Christ.*

A final source of worry for Raymond were Hedvig and Sven whom he felt worked too hard and worried about him too much. (Ernie expressed this concern in his letters as well.)

He just wanted things to be normal again—in his own life and in the lives of people at home.

While Raymond was plainly afraid of going overseas, he became so sick and tired of training, and the sameness of it all, that he thought he would welcome any kind of a change, even if the change included action. He talked himself into believing that a soldier actually has an easier time of it overseas than he does in training because, even though the action can get pretty tough, there comes a time when it's over and he can retire to a rear area and have peace for a while. In contrast, the demands of training almost guaranteed no time for rest and solitude. (Raymond's thinking compares with that of many war observers and writers who describe the combat infantrymen as resenting the men in their rear who slept safely at night, while the soldiers in the rear thought it an advantage to being on the front line and not having to deal with the minutia and boredom of the rear.)

Raymond was among the 90 percent of the men in uniform who never got anywhere near the fighting, so he didn't think the country owed him anything. He believed that America won the war at least partly because officers and soldiers weren't afraid to question authority and came up with their own plan if they didn't think the one handed to them was going to work. He contrasted the American soldier to the German soldier who *blindly follows orders*, and he admired American soldiers who refused to be intimidated by officers. *When they meet an officer face to face, they don't even bother to salute. And if the officer stops and gives them a tail chewing they grin right in his face. There isn't much the brass hats can do about it either. Those guys have been through so much they don't feel like humbling themselves to any officer who has never even seen a battlefield.*

Camp Maxey, Texas
May 5, 1945
Dear Mother,

Well, now that Mother's Day is soon here I am going to write you a letter, Mom, to wish you health and happiness on Mother's Day. I was going to send you a card but by the time I got around to go over and buy one they were all sold out. So I am going to send you a few lines instead. How are you getting along, Mom? Are you feeling okay? I sure hope you are. I have been thinking a lot about you since I got in the army and I realize more and more what a wonderful mother you have been to me. When I think of all the times you laid awake at night worrying about us guys when we were out on all those sprees, I sure feel ashamed of it, Mom. And then all the worry about Ernie you had to go through. I know you didn't sleep very much at all during his illness. I've been wondering what do you think Ernie would have been when he grew up? He would be 29 years old now. I know you still think about him a lot, Mom. It sure is a shame he had to die so young. You and I both cried for him and I know that you still sometimes cry. I couldn't use his rifle for a long time after he died. I still think about him when I go hunting.

So I want to say that I'm sorry I caused you so much worry when I was home. A guy doesn't realize such things until you get in the mess I'm in now. It takes the army to wake a man up. If I ever get back home, Mom, it's going to be different.

Well, how are things going at home? I suppose the boys haven't started in the fields yet. Myrtle wrote that you are having tough weather up there. That sure is too bad if it keeps up. I suppose the spring work will get awful late. There isn't much rain down here. The dust keeps blowing in your face all the time so at night I look more black than white.

I hear the boys are getting a lot of nice lumber. The logs on the south pile must have been some dandies. I told some of the guys about that log that yielded so many 2x4s and they sure thought that was dandy. Those guys believe that Northern Minnesota is a real wilderness and I don't say anything to change their minds.

The sergeant that has charge of the 4th platoon that I'm in is one of the nicest men that I've ever had the privilege to meet. He doesn't even have a temper. And he's one of the smartest trainers in the camp. He told us when he first took over the platoon that if we cooperate with him he'll make us the best trained platoon in the whole battalion. And I believe he can do that. He said, "I know you guys don't like the army and I sure don't blame you either because I don't like it myself." But he said we have a job to do and the more we get down to brass tacks and train hard the sooner we'll all get back home where we want to be. He expects to be shipped out himself as soon as this training cycle is over. If I have to go into the real thing I sure would want to have him telling me what to do when a tight squeeze comes.

Tomorrow is Sunday and I had hoped to get the day off but an order just came from the company commander that a detail has to go out on the rifle range and do some work. My name is on that list so I'll have to work on Sunday. The last time we went to the rifle range we spent a whole week out there sleeping in tents in blazing heat. It was one of the worst weeks of my life.

God bless you, Mom, and don't worry about me. Tell the boys to write regular because I sure look forward to letters. I get so happy when my name is called during mail call. It's usually at chow time so I have to eat before I can read my letter. But I'm telling you it doesn't take me long to shovel that swill down and get back to my barracks. I don't think there's nothing better to brace up a lonely soldier than to get a letter from home. You should see the guys' faces when they get a letter. It brightens up a lot. I always feel sorry for those who don't get letters and there are many who don't.

Pray for me, Mom, and tell Dad and my brothers to pray for me also, because now is when I need God's help more than ever. Tell Roy thanks a lot for his letter and I'll write to him as soon as time will permit. I know he and Margaret are getting married on June 30. I wish him a lot of happiness. Margaret is a peach of a girl. I only hope the kid gets down to brass tacks and realize that life is something more than just having fun. I know that God will bless his marriage. Myrtle says that my little Jean prays for her Daddy every night and I'm sure that God will hear her innocent prayers and bring me home safely to her.

Love from your son,
Raymond

Pvt Raymond Pearson
37794397 Company A
108th ITB; 27th ITR IRTC
Camp Maxey, Texas

The letters Raymond welcomed most were those from Sven and Hedvig who wrote infrequently, probably because they couldn't write in English and were embarrassed by that fact. Hedvig wrote in Norwegian and Sven in Swedish. Raymond was able to read and enjoy the letters in both languages. *There's something in letters from your Mother and Dad that means a lot to a guy. When I read your letter, Pa, I shed the first tears since I got in the army. And I thought I had gotten to be what the army wants all men to be— hard as a rock. But thank God, I found out that I wasn't so hard.*

It's been said that war is a team sport. From the private on up, soldiers learn to take orders and do as they're told. They are trained together to trust and depend on one another, knowing that's how it will be in combat. They become friends. It's also been said that military training takes away a person's concept of his own individualism and replaces it with a strong sense of shared responsibility as a member of a team. This transformation is important in order to survive in combat. Raymond doesn't appear to have been transformed in this way, however; at least there's no evidence of that happening in his letters. He maintained his individualism throughout training and, while he nurtured friendships with the Minnesota guys and developed some new ones, it's not clear he ever thought of himself as that integer in a team. His basic characterization of training was weeks and weeks of hard work and monotony—how to follow orders and shoot a gun only to witness the exact opposite of what he was told to do. The monotony, hard work, and a basic fear of going overseas before the war ended presented a challenge for him. However, it was his homesickness and nostalgia for a way of life he was now learning to appreciate that most likely created whatever bond he felt with his fellow soldiers.

How Raymond really felt about serving his country is difficult to know. His attitude alternated between harboring an intense dislike for the Army and its rules and accepting his fate, even admiring certain elements of army life, such as officers who didn't abide by the rules. He hated the war but decided that he wanted to be a good soldier. He was worried about the army turning him into a hard-boiled person and that may have been his greatest concern, aside from getting killed without his heart being right with God.

Most of Raymond's letters ended with the same exhortation that Ernie used in his letters: *Don't worry about me, Mom, because I'm getting along okay. So long for this time and God be with you till we meet again.*

The war in Europe was ending. Shortly after Raymond wrote his first letter from Camp Maxey, Texas, on April 18, 1945, the final battles were being fought, Hitler committed suicide, and Germany surrendered on all fronts. When Americans awakened to the news of Germany's unconditional surrender on May 8, 1945, they assumed that the whole world was at peace. President Truman corrected that assumption with the reminder that the West was free, but the East still lay in the hands of the Japanese who refused to surrender.[16]

As news of the surrender broke in the West, and the war in the Pacific intensified, Raymond was still talking about going overseas to fight in combat. In a letter written on June 19th he said, *I talked with Lester about going overseas and you ought to see the sick look on his face. I guess he's plenty scared too and I don't blame him. They show us so many actual combat films that are taken right on the worst battlefields of the war and they are scaring the wits out of the guys. I suppose the army wants to prepare us for some of the horrors over there. I only hope that in some way this terrible war will end before I have to go over.*

The whole weight of the Allies was now thrown against Japan. Raymond, and everyone else in his company, knew that the war in Europe was over, but, because the war in the Pacific was growing, the level of intensity of their training didn't change. Raymond was concerned about all of the discharges the Army was giving, presumably because it felt that Japan could be defeated with a smaller army. He didn't think that was a valid assessment of Japan's power and it worried him. *I think Japan is plenty tough and they're counting on bombing her into submission.*

Raymond loved to talk to soldiers and officers who had spent time in fighting zones and who were willing to share their thoughts about how the war was going. For example, a soldier who had fought at Guadalcanal visited the camp and Raymond listened to him talk about how Guadalcanal was a horrific battle for the American soldiers who were not used to the jungle environment. He described how the screams of the birds, macaws and parrots, were nerve-wracking because the Japanese imitated those bird sounds so the Americans lived in a constant state of tension. *I sure like to talk to those boys who have spent months in the jungles. They can give a guy the lowdown on the Japs and they say if anyone tells us the Japs can't fight, he's a liar. Those soldiers are really tough.*

In April, he wrote about the conversations he had had with some officers who expressed hope that Russia would go against Japan. If this should happen, they reasoned, the war wouldn't last long because Russia was rated as one of the strongest countries in the world, earning its reputation after the Battle of Stalingrad, when the Russians destroyed the German 6th Army during that horribly cold winter a couple of years ago. When Germany finally surrendered on February 2, 1943, the Battle of Stalingrad was considered its greatest defeat. It was a decisive Soviet victory and a turning point of the war in Europe.[17]

While the American officers Raymond was talking to expressed admiration for the Russians who forced Germany to surrender, they were also nervous about Russia and communism. Raymond, however, couldn't hold back his enthusiasm.

Boy, I sure hope those Reds roll across the Manchurian border and give the Japanese some of the medicine Germany got in the Battle of Stalingrad. They tell us there will be no invasion of Japan or China until the Japanese fleet and Air Force are completely knocked out. Then it shouldn't be so hard to give those Japs a good trouncing.

In another letter, Raymond wrote that *the way the news looks it shouldn't take so long before we invade Japan. And with the overwhelming sea and air power we've got, it shouldn't be so hard to make a landing. The reason the fighting has gone so slow on these islands is because we were not able to use heavy equipment. But once we can get the tanks rolling it won't last long. At least that's what the brass hats tell us. I hope they know what they're talking about.*

One thing that never seemed to worry Raymond was the opinion of others. He enjoyed a good argument, especially one that put him in the minority. In that sense, he was something of a maverick. In a conversation about the possibility of a war between the United States and Russia, he had no compunction about telling his fellow soldiers that a war with Russia was one he would never fight. As a result, he was called a Communist, but the label didn't bother him at all. In fact, he said *I get a kick out of stirring things up, especially when I think that these guys are being stupid in the things they say. They're so scared of Communism they think that Russia will take over the world if we let them. I don't believe that and I don't mind telling them so.*

July 13, 1945
Dear Mother, Dad and Brothers

Well, evening is here again and I have just finished cleaning up my equipment so now I have nothing to do the rest of the evening. I am going to try and get together a few lines again. How are you all getting along? How are you, Mom and Pop? I suppose you are both busy as usual. I'll bet the garden looks as nice as ever. I've always said when it comes to getting a nice garden I've never seen the equal to yours. I sure hope you've planted plenty of tomatoes this year because when I come home on furlough they should be ripe and I sure am going to do full justice to them. We get a lot of tomatoes in the army but they have been kept in cold storage so long they taste like the dickens.

We sure have had some tough training lately. Bayonet every day and that is one kind of training that takes a lot of endurance. It wouldn't be so bad if it wasn't for this awful heat every day. But the way we have to dress with these heavy fatigue jackets and never get a chance to roll up our sleeves just makes it tough. You should have seen me after I got through with the Bayonet Obstacle Course. Every bit of my clothing was soaking wet from sweat. And when you have got this prickly heat it sure makes it miserable but it can't last so much longer now so I guess I'll pull through. If this doesn't toughen a man up I guess nothing will. I guess we don't realize how lucky we are to live up in Northern Minnesota. I've seen quite a bit of country since I left home but I wouldn't trade Roseau County for all the other counties in the union.

I heard that tomorrow we're going to be issued light clothing because we're moving out around 5:00 for bivouac and then it will be two weeks before I sleep under a roof again. It's going to be pretty rough out there because of the heat. There are a lot of fellows that have been overheated and have had to go to the hospital. But I'm going to make it if it kills me because if I don't make it this time I'll have to do it all over again and I want to get home now more than anything else in the world. After I come in from bivouac I'll only have a few weeks left so I should be home around the first of September. Oh Happy Day.

This morning the Chaplain came out in his jeep and held a meeting for us and he had a young lieutenant with him. All the guys that were interested gathered under a big hickory tree and we sang songs and the Chaplain prayed in his lifeless way. Then the young lieutenant got up to preach and I sat there spellbound. I never thought that I would see a man in this tough army that really had the love of God in his heart. I sure feel happy today.

I just got a letter from Roy and Margaret and Roy said you were still haying. The weather must have gone haywire up there. That's the only thing I can think of that's wrong with Roseau County—too much rain. But to me it's still the best place in the world. I know one thing when I come back there to stay I don't care if it rains or freezes. I'm going to be satisfied. I think I was meant to go through the army to make me appreciate what I've got at home.

A guy hasn't anything to kick about as long as he is free.

Well, at 3:00 today we are pushing off for a Combat Range where we are to start using live ammo. It's about five miles from where we are camped now so it isn't very far. But the heat today is terrific. The sun is blazing down and it's so sultry I can hardly breathe. And we have to carry a full field pack and our rations. This is the toughest life I've ever lived in but it won't last long now. Boy, I sure will be glad to say goodbye to this country. The poor guys that died at the Alamo sure didn't die for much if you ask me.

When I get home, Mom, you better have that table set with a lot of good things to eat because this boy of yours is pretty hungry for some of your home cooked food. I have thought more than once about that wonderful potato soup you used to make when I was home. When you compare the soup these army cooks slap together with yours there just isn't any comparison. I remember Ernie always talking about your potato soup in his letters. He said it was the best in the world. I have to agree with that. If I remember, he said that he wanted his friend in the hospital to have some of your soup. I wonder what happened to him.

Well, I suppose I had better quit before you play your eyes out reading this long letter. I think I will go up to the CX and get myself some ice cream with that dollar I got from you. I was flat broke before I got that so thanks a lot for it. May God bless you all.

Love, Fat

For a period of time, Raymond was so convinced by the stories of those who had received discharges from the Army that he believed he could qualify for one. He applied for an agricultural discharge on the advice of another guy in the Army who had had a lawyer write a letter to the company commander. It was a sworn and notarized statement of how much land and stock this guy had. Raymond checked with his commanding officer who told him that if he wrote a letter stating five reasons why he should get a discharge, the CO would start the ball rolling. Raymond wrote the letter, trying to convince his CO (and the draft board) that he qualified for a discharge from the Army. Later, a friend told him that he had overheard the CO and another officer talking about Raymond's application, and it was his opinion that Raymond would most likely get the discharge because of his age. So the next morning Raymond signed the papers and was told that the final decision was up to the local board and some big shots in Washington.

Well, a couple of weeks later, Raymond got the news that his application for an agricultural discharge was turned down. The Army officials said it was because the letter he wrote to the commanding officer wasn't convincing; it didn't provide a powerful enough argument for granting a discharge. They said he could try again, but Raymond didn't think it was any use.

By the time I got another letter written and sent in and it had made the rounds the training period would be over and I know for a fact after they have spent so much time training a man to make a soldier out of him they are not going to let him go unless there is an ironclad reason. So I guess I had better stop trying to kid myself about getting out of the army. I am a soldier now and I guess I will be one for the duration. I guess it sounds like I'm yellow when I say that I don't want to go across, but the idea goes against me. It's not just that I'm scared, but what bothers me most is this training to kill. I know it is entirely against my conscience because it isn't right to take another man's life, but I'm in so deep now there isn't much I can do about it. Today we practiced combat formation. That's learning signals the Platoon leaders use when we advance upon the enemy and learning how to disperse so we won't be bundled up when we run into enemy fire. When I get really down I think about home and our place out east. I can close my eyes and see our little house any time I want to. When the day comes and I can go home and be with my little family again I'll be the happiest guy in the world.

Raymond wanted a discharge, but when he was denied one, he accepted the decision as an indication that he was supposed to serve his country. From that point on, he redefined himself as a good soldier, and he no longer had such a fear of the future that had plagued him since he was drafted. *I've had this awful fear of the future.... was so afraid of going across and fighting that I tried to get myself discharged from the Army. But now I'm going to trust God and not fear anything. I'm going to start preparing myself to go across because I know that the same God that keeps me safe on this side of the ocean can also keep me safe over there.*

Interspersed throughout his letters were many references to Raymond's distaste for being trained to kill his fellow man. There was also reference to the nervousness he felt about fighting the Japanese whom the American soldiers thought of as not only tough, but fanatical in their determination to keep on fighting, even when they knew they couldn't win. They were willing to fight with no hope or purpose, something the American soldiers said they wouldn't do. One of the guys in Raymond's unit read parts of letters he received from his brother, a Marine who had fought on Peleliu and Okinawa where casualties rocketed and hatred from both sides soared to a new level. His brother said that when the Marines injured Japanese soldiers they had to kill them because if they tried to help them, the Japanese would detonate a grenade to kill one last Marine.

Raymond and his fellow soldiers probably wouldn't have been so astonished at the words of the Marine letter writer if they had known that the Japanese were taught from early in their lives to believe in their nation's imperial destiny. They were taught to revere honor and dignity above all else, so that when they became soldiers, they were willing to sacrifice everything—ideals, honor, even their families—for the Emperor and his war. The Japanese soldier was to fight valiantly with no hope of survival. He wouldn't be taken prisoner, so the only choice the Americans had was to exterminate him on the battlefield.[18]

Today we saw a film taken on Iwo Jima of actual bayonet fighting. The film showed Japs and Doughboys locked in hand to hand combat and at least 10 Japs were killed. I can't see how the Japanese can stand up at all against the Americans. And the Americans' faces looked hardly human when they stabbed the Japs to death. This war is a terrible thing and I wish I didn't have to be a part of it. To think that we have to kill people that we have nothing against and have never seen before. It's horrible. I know that Pearl Harbor started the war with the Japanese but I still wish we didn't have to kill so many men in such horrible ways.

Raymond's disgust with the war was so great that at one point he refused to accept a sharpshooter medal for shooting the M1. He said that the Army could keep his medal because he would never wear it. *Maybe I'll send it home to the little Jammer* (Jean) *so she can play with it. Then maybe I shouldn't do that. I don't want her to think that there is anything good about this war.*

At the end of July, after the Americans had beaten the military power of Japan on Okinawa, the big three leaders—Truman, Churchill, and Stalin— met and demanded that Japan unconditionally surrender. The Japanese ignored the American ultimatum, so President Truman felt that he had no choice but to use the atom bomb. On August 6th, the United States bombed Hiroshima, rationalizing that the horrific act would save thousands of American lives. Maybe the bombing did save those lives, but it also killed 100,000 Japanese. Truman once again warned Japan to surrender and, when he received no response, gave the order to bomb Nagasaki on August 9th. Less than a week later, Japan surrendered. Now, with both a victory in Europe and a victory in Japan, the whole world was finally at peace.[19]

In one of the last letters he wrote from Camp Maxey, Raymond talked about the end of the war and his initial reaction to the atomic bomb. *Well, the way it looks this war is going to end at last. Russia is driving forward in her usual manner and that atom bomb is raising havoc so the way they say it is only a matter of a few days. Won't that be wonderful to see this war end. Then the killing will stop and all of us homesick guys can go home Some of us are going to be shipped overseas for guard duty or reconstruction work because I hear the U.S. is going to help build up some of the war-torn countries. But that won't be bad.... Some of the officers were telling us about how the atomic bomb works. They said that it melts steel and forms it into a gas so it floats around in the air. This must be getting to be Buck Rogers days. The way science is making progress if we ever have another war it will be the wiping out of civilization.*

Raymond quickly lost his fascination with the atom bomb after he learned more details of its potential for destruction. He was definitely conflicted by the bombing of Hiroshima and Nagasaki. His compassion and strong sense of morality produced feelings of injustice and disgust for the American government and especially Truman who made the decision to drop the bombs.

Just think, we now have the capability with this terrible nuclear weapon to destroy thousands of innocent lives. Some of the guys are saying that the Japanese weren't even warned about the bomb, that the U.S. warned them they would be attacked but they didn't say it would be an atomic bomb. Maybe the Japanese government would have surrendered if they had known. I can't believe it was necessary. So many thousands of people killed and who knows how many will die from all that radiation. Think of what a horrible death. President Truman will have a lot to answer for some day for making that decision.

In another letter, however, he expresses a different opinion. *Most of the guys support the bombings. They say that it caused the Japanese to surrender so we didn't have to attack them. And if we had invaded Japan, there would have been much greater casualties on both sides. The Japanese are tough though. One sergeant said they wouldn't have surrendered even if they had known the attack was going to be an atomic bomb.*

In letters that followed, it is apparent that Raymond was so greatly distressed by the conflicting opinions regarding the bombing of Japan that he could think of little else for a while. He ultimately decided that it was probably the right decision to bomb Hiroshima, but there couldn't be any ethical justification for dropping the second bomb and repeating the terrible damage and death toll. It was inherently immoral.

He wondered about the *guy who dropped the bomb. Did he ever stop to think about what happened when the bomb connected? Or didn't he have to think about that at all since he never had to see people die?* Paul Tibbets, who dropped the first atomic bomb to be used in the history of warfare ("Little Boy") on Hiroshima, said that he knew he had a job to do and he did it.

He also questioned God's role in this, something he didn't do very often. *How could God allow this to happen? It makes no sense that he would allow the horrible death of so many innocent people with just one plane dropping one bomb, Innocent people get killed in wars all of the time but this is different. There were just too many killed in an instant with no warning.*

He ended one letter with this: *Mom, you always told us that we shouldn't question God's wisdom. Even when Ernie died you didn't question God. I suppose I shouldn't do that now but it's hard to understand how God could permit this terrible thing.*

Along with the horror he felt toward the bombing of Japan, Raymond also believed that our country's treatment of the Japanese-Americans during the war was shameful. Two months after Pearl Harbor, 120,000 Americans of Japanese ancestry living in military exclusion zones on the West Coast were forced to leave their homes within 48 hours and relocate to one of ten internment camps where they lived in barracks and had communal eating and bathing. Completely focused on winning the war, President Roosevelt succumbed to the pressure applied on him by state representatives who felt there was a danger of these Americans spying for the Japanese. Because of war hysteria that had seized the country, Japanese Americans lost their civil liberties and endured the trampling of their values—all the while Japanese units were fighting hard against the Germans. *How the Japanese can ever forgive the Americans for this, I'll never know.*[20]

The other injustice of which Raymond was aware and commented on in his letters was the discrimination against black soldiers in the army. He heard guys talking about African-Americans who wanted to fight but were relegated to noncombat positions, such as cooks and guards. These servicemen suffered discrimination even when they ventured off base to surrounding towns.

(Note: While discrimination and segregation existed in the Armed Forces during World War II, eventually the realities of war blurred racial lines, and progress was made to correct the situation, at least in part due to the continuing intervention of Eleanor Roosevelt.

Between 1940 and 1945, the black military force had increased in size from 5,000 to 920,000, and the number of black officers had grown from five to over 7,000. In the Battle of the Bulge alone, 2,000 black soldiers volunteered to fight. Also, by the end of the war, black soldiers held jobs in almost every branch of the Army as artillerymen, infantrymen, paratroopers, and more. So, progress in attaining true equality for black soldiers was slow, but, eventually, they were on equal footing with white soldiers.)[21]

Camp Adair, Oregon
(September 20-October 8, 1945)

It's September and Raymond is in Camp Adair, having returned from a two-week furlough on the farm in Minnesota. For the month that he was there, he mostly played a waiting game, not knowing if he was going to be sent overseas and if he were, wishing he knew where he would be stationed.

But first, he describes his trip from Roseau, Minnesota to Camp Adair, Oregon, which he classifies as a nightmare on a series of trains and busses. After five days and six nights of little sleep and even less activity, he arrived at the Camp two days late and so stiff he could hardly stand up to salute when he went before the Court Martial officer who demanded an explanation.

I thought it was no use to lie so I told him that I never thought it would take so long to get here and I didn't leave home on time. He said I'd have to go up for a hearing. I'm not too worried because I've talked to guys who have been late and all they had to do was pay *a $14 fine. The thing that gets my goat though is that I wouldn't have been late if I had taken a different route. I would have been here by Sunday and I could have turned my GI ticket in and had every cent I paid out for fare refunded. But that's the way it goes when a guy doesn't know the ropes.*

I don't know where Al or any of the Roseau guys are. They had all been here at the Receiving Depot and were assigned to outfits before I got here. So I sure lost out by being late. I hope I can find out what outfit they're in so I can see them but if I don't I'll find some new guys to knock around with. That's one thing about the army, it's easy to make friends.

He was grateful for the opportunity of seeing beautiful scenery from nine states as he traveled across the country but *a guy can't enjoy it the way he should when every turn of the wheels takes you further away from home.* It was tough for him to leave the place he loved for a second time.

So now he's reduced to waiting, still hoping that he won't be sent across but knowing there is little chance of that happening. *We are all equipped for overseas service now so I suppose it's just a matter of time. A whole battalion shipped out yesterday. They've issued me so much clothes and equipment I don't know what to do with it all. They have always said when the American soldier goes overseas he is the best equipped soldier in the world and I can see now why they say that. Everything they give you is new stuff and all the clothes are checked so they fit perfectly. We had a physical exam for overseas but as usual they couldn't find anything wrong with me so I guess my goose is cooked—again.*

While Raymond was waiting to go somewhere, he was looking for clues to his destination. His hope was that he would be sent to the Japanese mainland instead of to some island in the Pacific, which he felt would be a pretty lonesome existence. Evidence seemed to be mounting, however, that suggested he wouldn't get his wish. For example, he heard that the Army needed 100,000 troops to occupy all of the islands *so a guy stands a pretty good chance of getting sent to one of them.... We have been having so much instruction on the control of malaria so I think we'll go to some tropical zone.* Not much later he wrote that a lieutenant told them about the 175,000 troops waiting to be relieved in the Philippines, so Raymond thought that he might end up there. *I would much sooner go there than I would to Japan. At least a guy would be among friendly people.*

Raymond thought that the guessing was over when he received his orders to ship out the next day. But in the last minute when he was about to be given his equipment, he and twelve other guys were taken off the shipping list. Those who remained on the list were given shots for the kinds of diseases one would expect to find in a cold climate. Raymond didn't know the reason for the change, just that he wouldn't be going across with his company. At that moment, he had a glimmer of hope that he wouldn't be sent overseas, but common sense told him that this was just a stay and the move was inevitable.

While the Army remained mysterious in terms of destinations for overseas assignments, the morale of the soldiers was becoming increasingly low. *You ought to hear the guys bellyache about being in the army. They're getting so they don't care about anything. I haven't seen one man clean his rifle since I got here, and that's one job that's supposed to be done every day. So you can tell the Army is losing its power over the soldiers.*

Morale was bolstered temporarily by the arrival of a soldier who was recently discharged from the Army, having been in the service for more than five years. He talked about fighting across France and Belgium, participating in the Battle of the Bulge, then moving into Germany and Czechoslovakia. The men in Raymond's unit had never seen any fighting and were fascinated by the stories of someone who had been in the thick of the war until the end.

It was fall, Raymond's favorite season in Minnesota where *the leaves must be golden brown by now and the whitetails are nice and plump. And soon it will be time to string the steel and get the mink line going again.... this is the toughest time of the year to be in the Army. I don't think it's quite so bad in the summer when there isn't much hunting. But in the fall when a guy's trigger finger just naturally gets itchy and I picture myself along the swamp edge on the ridge with the old black pot over the fire and not a care in the world, I feel pretty blue. But I'll have to try and steer my thoughts away from such dreams or I'll be going over the hill and that's something that doesn't pay in the Army.* He must have been feeling unusually homesick at that time, a feeling exacerbated by the uncertainty about his future in the Army.

Finally, the day arrived when Raymond knew he would be shipped out. Apparently, the Army was closing Camp Adair down, and by the end of October there wasn't to be a soldier left in the Camp. *All the guys with 36 points and over are to be shipped to other camps and the guys that are short points are taking that long voyage. So I figure that sometime next week I'll be on the Banana Boat.*

He was ready to go. He figured that as long as he had to go anyway, he might as well get on board with the next phase of his Army life. It wasn't much fun, lying around not knowing what's going to happen from one day to the next. Besides, they were still supposed to be in training, which wasn't going well because of the morale and fitness problems with the men. There was the time that the CO blew his top, and selected one of his "Athletic Louies" to take them out for three miles of road work. They ran two miles and were so played out and stiff the next day they could hardly walk. And they were supposed to be trained soldiers! Raymond felt that he redeemed himself a little when he *smacked the ball a terrific wallop* during a softball game. He allowed as how it might have been a home run if he had been in shape.

On October 8, 1945, Raymond wrote a letter to Hedvig wishing her a Happy Birthday. He had just been put on shipping orders and the orders said direct shipment overseas. At that time he thought he was heading across the Pacific and wanted to reassure his mother that he would be safe: *Don't worry about me, Mom. If I take care of myself there's no reason why anything should happen to me now that the War is over.*

I've never in my life seen so many dissatisfied men as there are now in the Army. They all want to go home. Every morning at roll call there are four or five guys missing—A.W.O.L. They don't seem to care what the Army does to them. I guess homesickness has got the best of them. For my part, I can't see any sense in doing that. The army takes all your pay and allowances away and makes it twice as hard for you to get out. So I'm going to stick it out unless I keep losing weight so I'm nothing but a shadow of who I was before I enlisted. Ernie would get a good laugh out of that. What a pair we made! He was so skinny and I was pretty hefty growing up. If this keeps up, I'll lose my nickname.

I've been thinking about Ernie again. It seems like you and Ernie are together in my thoughts a lot of the time, Mom. I remember how he trusted me to keep his animals and his gun okay. And he was always telling me to help you. All he wanted was to get well so that he could be on the farm with all of us again. Seems to me that could have happened.

How are the boys doing with the threshing? I heard it's been raining a lot there. I hope the crops aren't too damaged. I had hopes of making enough off my oats to fix the house this fall so Myrt and Jean can keep staying there. I'm glad to hear that Joan has been staying with Jean so they can play together.

Don't let Myrtle stay alone too much so she has time to think about our situation too much. You should see the letters I get from Jean. She sure is getting good to write.

Happy Birthday, Mom, and may you have many more. Greet Pa and the boys. Promise not to worry about me.

*Love your son,
Raymond*

Fort Ord, California
(October 12-November 1, 1945)

For reasons unknown, Raymond wasn't shipped across the ocean, at least not right away. When Camp Adair closed down, he was sent to Fort Ord in California. His two-week sojourn there was marked by four decisions (in quick sequence): enlist in the Regular Army, not enlist, try for another discharge, and enlist (again). There were times when Raymond's life was anything but dull!

The first letter he wrote home upon arrival at Fort Ord was filled with his decision to enlist in the Regular Army for a year. *I know this might sound kind of screwy to you but here's the way I got it figured. If I went across right now without enlisting I might have to stay over there for a lot longer than a year. But if I enlist now I'll be out in a year's time. After I get my discharge down here I get $200 mustering out pay and five cents a mile for traveling pay. Right after I'm discharged I enlist in the regular army 24 hours later and then I get a 30-day furlough so I'll be home in time for hunting season. It sure is going to be wonderful to get home especially this time of the year. I never thought I would* *make it for hunting this year, but it now looks like I'll be on post while the bombardment starts on the ridge.*

He then goes on to tell the story of his buddy, Marcelle Lockapelle, who could rightfully get out of the army because he had a wife and three kids. However, he planned on signing up for three years. *I asked him what in the world he wanted to be in the army that long for and he told me that he gets his choice of what branch of service he wants to be in and he can stay in the States. He gets $160 a month counting his pay and the allowance his wife and kids get. And he said it would be hard to find a job that's so easy as the peace time army and make that much money. So he plans on taking his family with him when he comes back from furlough and have them live near where he's stationed.*

Raymond ended that letter by describing the view he has out of the barracks window—the Pacific Ocean stretched out as far as he could see until a blanket of fog hanging over the water prevented him from seeing any more. *The ships out there look pretty small and when I think of crossing 4000 miles of that ocean I don't have much heart for that.*

A week later, Raymond wrote home that his decision to enlist in the regular army for a year was off, thanks to the Army breaking its promises. Apparently, he was under the impression that his unit was going to be at Camp Ord only for a few days and then would be sent home on furlough. After the men were settled, however, they were told that they might have to stay there for two months of advanced training. When Raymond heard this news, he told the CO that he wanted to withdraw his application for enlistment. The CO said that it was okay to withdraw since he hadn't signed anything, but he reminded Raymond that he would be transferred to an overseas regiment and shipped across.

Raymond's explanation of how he made the decision to withdraw his application went like this: *I told him if I had to hang around here for two months and then go home on that thirty day furlough and then come back and serve that year, I would be losing too much time because I figure I won't be across more than eight months.* The CO told him that he was probably right, so now Raymond is waiting for shipping orders again. But he is immensely relieved that he saved himself from spending unnecessary time in the Army. *I was nuts in the first place to even think of enlisting for one year in this darn army. When a guy once signs up and has served his enlistment term if the army wants to hold you longer all they have to do is put a little pressure on Congress. And they can hold a regular army man as long as they want to. So I'm glad that I realized this in time. None of that stuff for me.*

In his next weekly letter home, Raymond is trying to get out of the Army again. This time he's fighting for a dependency discharge (his former fruitless attempt involved an agricultural discharge). His rationale was that there are so many young married guys like him who were getting out of the Army every day because of dependents that he couldn't see why he shouldn't qualify. But the process he wanted to implement was so complicated that it's hard to believe anyone could have made it happen. First, Dr. Berge in Roseau had to write a letter attesting to the fact that Myrtle wasn't well (she hadn't been feeling well for some time). Then, Myrtle had to write a letter stating that she was not able to make ends meet on $80 a month with doctor bills and child expenses. And Hedvig was supposed to get a petition started and notarized to the effect that Raymond was needed at home, and then obtain a number of reliable signatures. But the requirement that consigned his chances for a discharge to the realm of the impossible was that Myrtle had to find him a job because, in order to get a discharge, he had to provide the Army with proof that work would be waiting for him at home. He suggested that Myrtle contact lumber owners in the area to see if one of them would write a letter saying that Raymond was an experienced woodsman who would be able to work for him. She was told not to contact Walter Hukee though, because he apparently was involved in Raymond's unsuccessful attempt to get an agricultural discharge.

When I told the Company Commander that I had changed my mind and I wanted to try for this dependency discharge instead, he looked a little skeptical but said that he would help me if I can get these papers down here in time, Mom. He said he wouldn't ship me out until the discharge has been disapproved. But I don't see why it should be disapproved.... I'm pretty sure that married guys like me won't be in the army long anyway. I almost made a bad mistake when I planned on signing up for a year. But it also saved me from going across right away.

Later that night, in the same letter, Raymond writes about the fun he had watching a long string of launches taking men from the big aircraft carrier, *Hornet*, into the town of Monterey. The *Hornet* was the sister ship of the *Hornet* that was sunk during the war and she had just come back from patrol in far eastern waters. Raymond was impressed with its size: *a real floating airfield.*

And now, for Raymond's fourth and final decision regarding the future of his Army career... .

Fort Ord, California
November 1, 1945
Dear Mom,

I received your letter today and it was so easy to read your Scandinavian. I wish you would write more often. I read that you are scared of this enlisting in the regular army. Well, Mom, I was kind of leery myself at first but now that I've studied it from all angles, I don't think I have anything to lose. I can't see any hope of getting out of the army in less than a year's time so I think if I sign up for a year I'm just as well off. If I would have used my head and thought about getting those papers when I was home I might have stood a chance of a dependency discharge but after I thought of it and sent you the letter from down here it was too late. This morning the army got moving. When we fell out for roll call this morning they told us we were going to enlist in the army today. The company commander gave us our choice. Enlist today or *be on the boat in three days. I decided I would sooner go home for a while first before I go over so I told the C.O. that I wanted my name put back on. I just didn't have the guts to ship across right now when I had a chance to go home first and I can't see the army shipping me across for less than a year anyhow. So I'm taking a chance. Today I was discharged from the draft army and signed my name on papers that puts me in the regular army for a year. Tomorrow we take the physical exam, the same kind we had when I was inducted. And on Saturday we draw our travel pay and our mustering out pay. On Monday, at noon, I board a bus right here in camp that will take me direct to Minneapolis. It's a special bus and does not stop for passengers along the road. Forty of us Minnesota guys chartered it for $32 a piece so it wasn't so bad after all. It's one of those big streamlined Greyhounds and it will take only four days to get to Minneapolis and I don't think that's so bad considering I'll be crossing the whole U.S. So you can look for me sometime next week. Don't write any more letters because I won't be here to get them. Greet Pa and the Boys. See you soon, Mom.*

Love your son,
Raymond

After a 30-day November furlough on the farm in Falun, Raymond stopped in Fort Snelling, Minnesota *en route* to Camp Pickett, Virginia. He wrote home to tell his family that he saw Jackie Graves beat Jimmy Joyce—three knockouts in the preliminaries—in a boxing match he watched with his cousin, Harold. He also told of his visit with his Uncle Ted who reminded Raymond of his father. Ernie's name was thrown about in several conversations, and Raymond enjoyed talking about his brother with people who had known him while he was hospitalized in Minneapolis.

Camp Pickett, Virginia
(January 1-January 7, 1946)

Raymond arrived at Camp Pickett on New Year's Eve with the expectation that he would be assigned a bunk and then be told to go out and celebrate. Instead, he and the other soldiers in his unit were taken over to the personnel affairs building for regular overseas processing. It wasn't until almost midnight when they were allowed to retire to their bunks.

We kept on till 11 o'clock last night and then they showed us a bunk. This morning they woke us at 5:30 and we had to march through a sea of red mud to a place where they hold roll call. After roll call they fed us some swill they called breakfast and then we started clothing check. Some guys asked the officer in charge what all the hurry was about and he said we were due to sail within a week so they had to hurry this shipment as much as possible. So the way it looks it won't be many days before I'll be sailing for foreign soil.

I'm sure we are due to go to Germany as this is an ETO camp on the Atlantic coast and they are taking our Suntans away from us and giving us warmer clothes so I guess that means a colder country than any place in the Pacific. I'm glad I'm going to the ETO as that is a lot better than the

Pacific. Boy! This sure has been some New Years celebration. I don't hardly realize that a new year has come in.

That day was January 1, 1946. It was the first day of a new year that arrived with no fanfare for the soldiers at Camp Pickett.

In the last months of the war in Europe and immediately after, American soldiers discovered the concentration camps that had been used by the Nazis for human extermination. Eight months after the discovery of the camps, Raymond, who was still stationed in the U.S. and waiting to go overseas wrote the following:

Yesterday they took us over and showed us a film in Germany. It was a real propaganda film showing all the concentration camps and the terrible things the Nazis did. I'm telling you it's so horrible that I don't want to give you the details. You wouldn't believe it. And you'd feel so bad about how people could do such horrible things to other people. It made me sick to watch. They told us when we get over there to show the Germans no mercy because if we treat them too soft, our kids will be fighting another war in 20 or 25 years. That sounds crazy to me because it wasn't the German people who fought in the war. The people are innocent. And the German army is so powerless now so I don't understand our orders to treat the Germans bad. Instead of knocking the German people around we should clean out all the big shots in the U.S. and Britain and then we'd probably have peace in the world. But in the army a guy can't say what he feels like or he'll be in the guard house for a real long stretch. It's going to be a swell day when a guy can get out of this mess and be a free man.

The rumors the men had been hearing about concentration camps were true. From 1939-1945, Hitler oversaw 15,000 camps where 14 million people were murdered by the Nazis. When the Allies arrived in the spring of 1945, they found 32,000 survivors in desperate need of medical care.

Despite reports of concentration camps and inhuman proceedings of the Third Reich, which was killing Jews and other "undesirables" in large numbers, FDR refused to believe the facts and was slow to respond. He believed that winning the war as quickly as possible was the best means of rescuing the Jews. Nevertheless, there is the belief that he could have tried harder by applying more pressure on Germany to release the Jews and by bombing the concentration camps, even if those steps saved only a few lives. As it was, President Roosevelt's inaction was costly for the whole world.[22]

Raymond ended his letter from Camp Pickett with his usual admonition to Hedvig and Sven: "Don't worry about me. There can't be much over there now." He was glad to be going to the ETO because the weather and people would be more of what he's used to. *There's one thing about going across. A guy will never forget that experience as long as he lives. And I'll get to see some country that I would never get to see otherwise. But I suppose I'll also see some pretty bad stuff too. A guy can't go over to Germany now and not expect to see a lot of suffering. I hope I can handle that.*

He thanked his mother for the two dollars she sent him. He was flat broke, having not gotten paid yet, and he'd run out of cigarettes so those two dollars came in handy. He also told Hedvig that by the time she receives his letter he will be sailing the high seas for lands heretofore unknown.

Boy, Mom, if you could see me tonight, you would have a good laugh. They told us today that we had to have GI haircuts before we ship so they took us by platoons over to the company barbershop. The barber took a look at my long thick hair and with a wicked grin on his face, he went to work. After I was done my hair was exactly a half inch long and it stands straight on my head. It sure is heck when a man can't have his hair the way he wants it, but that's the Army for you.

Camp Kilmer, New Jersey
(January 11-January 17, 1946)

Raymond spent about a week at Camp Kilmer before he was sent overseas. Only 36 miles from New York, he took advantage of the opportunity to visit the city. *No wonder it's called the biggest city in the world. All of the other cities I've been in seem pretty small alongside New York. I strolled down the Great White Way and I've never seen so many people and lights in my life. I saw the Empire State Building and that building is really high—102 stories. Everything you're going to buy is sky high. A little bottle of beer is 40 cents and a decent meal is a dollar or a dollar and a half. I* *paid $4 for the cheapest room I could find in Times Square so a poor GI can't have much fun in a town like that, but at least I can say that I've been in New York. I remember Ernie talking about that kid Tom in the hospital with him. He really liked New York and that was during Prohibition when alcohol was illegal but still abundantly available in New York. I think it would have been a good time to be in this city then.*

The soldiers were on the alert—restricted to their barracks, having had all of their equipment inspected for the last time—knowing that at any minute they would be shipping out to Germany. Raymond views the prospect of going overseas with a mixture of uncertainty (*I only hope that it isn't too rough . . .*) and anticipation (*It makes a guy feel excited about crossing thousands of miles of ocean*!). He dreaded the shots that were forthcoming. *Those Army horse doctors aren't very gentle. They just sink the needle into the hilt and if you protest they tell you that you're a baby or some other smart remark.*

He describes the New Jersey countryside to his parents and brothers. *The farm houses on these prosperous looking farms look like mansions but it's funny, no matter how nice the country is, it still isn't home. I don't think I'd trade my little home in northern Minnesota for the grandest place in the world.*

He ends his second (and last) letter from Camp Kilmer with the familiar plea: *There's one thing I want to ask you all at home and that is not to worry about me . . . . if I'm careful and watch my step there's no reason why I can't make it back okay. I'll write as soon as I land. So long for now and please don't worry. And thank you for your letter, Mom. I was sure happy to hear from you.*

January, 1946-October, 1946

On May 7, 1945, Germany surrendered and the war in Europe was over. Tens of millions had lost their lives. For the U.S. Army, the post-war occupation of Germany was a huge undertaking—a mission almost as important as the war itself.

The devastation of the Allied bombing raids on Germany was raw and evident when Raymond arrived in January, 1946. For the next nine months, he would be an "occupation soldier" whose presence was necessary for peace-keeping and rebuilding the country. When he arrived in Marburg, he was shown parts of a document that contained orders from German-American Relations. The document made it clear that the American occupational forces had to conduct themselves at all times so as to command the respect of the German people for themselves and for the United States. They were told, for example, that the Germans would always be watching them and the image they had to project was that of a good American soldier. Other parts of the document admonished the occupational forces to remember that Germany, though conquered, was still an enemy, carrying on an undercover war with the Americans. The American Forces were never to hurt the Germans, collectively or individually, and they should engage in acts of violence only when required by military necessity.

It was believed that many Germans considered the WWII defeat as only an interlude, a time to prepare for the next war.[23]

Raymond was skeptical of what he read because the warnings didn't match his first impression of the German people. It is true that he was greeted with appalling destruction brought on by four years of Hitler's wrath, and it unnerved him to see the rubble. But he found the will of the people to be amazing and their determination to prevail extraordinary. It was after he had been in country for a while that his admiration was mixed with some distrust.

What exactly did American occupation soldiers do in Germany after the war in Europe ended? In addition to keeping the peace, their presence was for securing the occupation zone, performing guard duty in POW and displaced person camps, policing the streets on the look-out for black marketers, and supervising the thousands of captured Nazi prisoners. For the most part though, they were helping the Germans rebuild their country under provisions of the Marshall Plan.

There was also the humanitarian side of the war to handle. Hundreds of thousands of Germans had no homes and little food. German soldiers were being processed out of their wartime state. Food needed to be cooked for the military personnel, and refugees coming back to Germany needed care. Germany was in ruins after the war ended, and the government was in shambles. There was a lot of infrastructure work that needed to be done.[24]

Raymond landed in LeHavre, France, at the end of January after eight days of rough ocean travel that resulted in a significant number of seasick soldiers, but he didn't feel a thing. When he stepped ashore, he saw unbelievable destruction.

The whole town looked like a 200 mile wind had hit it. All you could see was piles of rubble and shells of buildings standing here and there among the ruins. This is the seaport that the Americans bombed for days and had to take by storm before the Germans pulled out. After we left the dock we were loaded into big semi trainer trucks for the ride out to the camp. You should have seen the people. They lined the narrow muddy streets and the soldiers threw candy, gum and cigarettes to them. They dove right into the mud to pick it up. And it wasn't only the kids that did it either. Old women, girls and men young and old would have gladly gotten a mud bath for a pack of cigarettes. It sure is pitiful to see what war can do to people. I saw a girl walking along with her head held high and she really looked proud. She was fairly well-dressed too. My buddy threw a pack of Camels at her and you should have seen her. She leaped through the air and almost knocked over two old guys who had the same idea. All pride was forgotten when it came to a pack of precious cigarettes. I guess they can't get any of that kind of stuff over here. All I can say is if it's this tough in France it must be many times worse in Germany.

The kind-heartedness of the American GI was legendary. When a troop train stopped in a town, the population of the whole town would meet the train to beg for food and cigarettes. The GIs would give away all the cigarettes they had on them, so they had to go without until they could get to the Camp PX. Raymond noted that this sacrifice produced many grouchy, cigarette-addicted soldiers, he among them. By the time they arrived at the PX, he said he wanted a cigarette so badly he couldn't think straight.

One day he was musing about the intrepidness and resourcefulness of the GIs who made money selling cigarettes at three times the cost. Raymond allowed as how they could do that because the people had a lot of money but nothing to spend it on. *Due to the shortage of various things over here, every cigarette is worth at least a dollar. There are very strict regulations over here to prevent one from selling such rationed goods and I guess these regulations are necessary for the soldiers would sell everything they got if they weren't in effect. Inflation is a terrible thing and Americans should be glad that the OPA (*Office of Price Administration*) has done so much in curbing it. I keep thinking that all the other guys sell on the Black Market so why shouldn't I. I'll tell you why. With my luck, I'd get caught and the Army doesn't take kindly to guys who buy and sell on the Black Market. We got strict orders to turn in every cent of our American money. And if any man keeps his and trades with the Germans, there's a ten to twenty year sentence so I guess it doesn't pay to take the risk. Many do though.*

In the same letter, he talks about how 40 guys came down with scarlet fever on the ocean crossing and now they're all quarantined to a tiny area. *How any guy can get sick over here is a mystery to me, since the Army has shot us so full of dope that I cannot see how any sickness can get through our systems. But I guess diseases get tougher when there's been a war. Right now we're sleeping 16 men to a tent with only candles for light. Those are pretty close quarters.*

From France, Raymond was sent by train to various places in Germany: first to Marburg, and then on to Osterholtz-Scharmbeck, Backnang, Heilbronn, Ludwisburg, and Asperg, ending his tour in Bremerhaven. He was overseas for a total of nine months. What follows are letters containing his observations during the time he spent in the various post-war German cities.

Marburg, Germany

From 1942 to 1945, Marburg, a beautiful Renaissance city on a hill, served as a hospital with schools and government buildings converted into wards. By the spring of 1945, there were over 20,000 patients, mostly wounded soldiers. As a result of its designation as a hospital city, there was not much damage from bombings.[25]

February 6, 1946

Dear Mother, Dad and Brothers,

Well, here I am in Marburg. We arrived this morning after a very tough trip which lasted four days. Talk about a train. I'll never forget that ride if I live to be a hundred. We traveled an average of ten miles an hour, sometimes spending hours on sidings waiting for some other train. We had only C rations to eat and boy when you eat cold beans and meat out of a can for four days it gets pretty rough. We had a lot of sick guys on the trip—mumps, measles and scarlet fever. But so far I'm healthy as an ox. Do you remember Ernie always commenting on my appetite and health? He would say, "Fat, with your health and appetite you should be able to hunt all day and not get tired or hungry. But I usually did get both. Man, I still remember those hunting days with Ernie.

I sure was surprised when I saw this city. I expected to see this like all the rest of Germany, bombed to ruins. But this place has hardly been touched by bombs. It really is a beautiful city. I hadn't been here an hour before I was issued a carbine and put on guard. I had to guard the main entrance to the hotel where we're staying. The Germans make up all kinds of excuses to get in there. But we can't let them pass unless they have a pass to prove that they are employed in there or have some business to talk over with the C.O. They sure are easy to give orders to. All the fight is gone out of the German people. They smile at us and act like we're some special kind of guests instead of an occupying army. But I'm not trusting them too much. They seem almost too friendly to suit me.

The GIs sure have a time with the frauleins over here. I'm sure that any one of us can pick up the best looking woman in Germany for a carton of cigarettes. This evening the street where I was on guard was full of girls waiting for guys to pick them up. And it wasn't long before the khaki-clad wolves moved in. Most of them have been around the GIs so much they can talk English pretty well and they sure make use of what they know. If a guy has plenty of cigarettes to sell over here you could make yourself rich. I sold one carton for 200 marks which is 20 dollars in American money. The Germans will pay a dollar for a bar of soap and you can almost set your own price for coffee and sugar. I know I said that I wouldn't get involved with making money on the Black Market but the Army doesn't seem to enforce that rule, so I'm just as bad as the next guy. I don't do much of it though and I don't feel like I'm hurting anyone because the people who pay for things they want can afford it.

After we get processed here we get sent to our regular units That should be the last trip before the one that means the most, the one where I go up the gang plank for the trip home. I'm looking forward to that day with all my heart. I sure am glad that I enlisted. They say over here that all the R.A. men will get home when their enlistment is up but the guys who are in the draft army might have to stay two years or more. So I didn't lose a thing.

Well, my second turn at guard is soon here. I'm on from 10 to 12 tonight and then from 4-6 in the morning. So I'd better quit and get a wink of sleep before I go on. Don't worry about me. You know I'll be okay. I'll write more as soon as I get the chance.

Love from Fat

February 9, 1946

Raymond saw his name on a list of 500 soldiers who were due to ship out to Bremen, Germany's biggest seaport where all the supplies for the occupation forces came in from the States. He surmised that his job would be everlasting guard duty, which would probably not be easy given the animosity the Germans felt toward the Americans. *When you say something to one of them, they smile and act real friendly but when your back is turned it's a different story. And in a way you can't blame them. We know how we'd feel if the Germans would have taken over our country. Then what makes the German guys hate us even more is the fact that the GIs have almost completely taken over all the girls. I've seen more than once a girl leaving a young German flat to go with an American GI. So you sure can't blame them for hating us.*

Today we had to go out on a march through the city. I guess they do that every once in a while to impress the civilians. There were at least 2000 men marching through the streets. We held up traffic which made the Germans mad, but I guess we're the boss now. In this town, the army took over the swellest beer tavern and stopped all civilians from going in there. The GIs can raise all the cane they want to and the MPs guard the door to see that no harm can come to them. Some setup. If the army can make lasting peace doing it this way, I'll be surprised.

It's hard to tell that there had been a war here. The buildings are in good shape and the people have pretty fair clothes. But up around Bremen, where I'm going next, they were so heavily bombed that the story will be very different. I'm glad that I'm going to belong to an outfit so I won't get pushed around from place to place. I hope Myrtle and Jean are okay. For my part I'm in perfect health even though we have lots of scarlet fever at the depot. So don't worry about me.

February 12, 1946

Raymond was fed up with army life because of the restrictions under which the soldiers were placed while in France and Marburg. They weren't allowed to leave the camp because of a measles and scarlet fever epidemic. At least that's what the Army said. Raymond believed that the Army was afraid to turn the soldiers loose because there were too many of them. Living in a place surrounded by guards and looking at four walls all day was unbearable.

Last night I'd had about all I could stand. So me and my three buddies got past the guards and went up town just to have a change of scenery. But we didn't stay out long. As we were coming out of a store, we saw two MPs standing right in front of us. We tried to get around them but it was too late. They ordered us to get in a truck and we started back to our prison. We weren't going very fast through the town and I knew we were going to be court martialed, so I jumped out and got away. I heard the MPs yelling but they didn't know my name or number. I hightailed it back to camp and managed to get past the guards who were talking and smoking so they didn't see me. I knew I'd be okay because my buddies wouldn't squeal. But they are in a bad spot along with 80 other guys. I guess I won't try that again. There's no choice but to just wait for my freedom.

The more I see of this country in Europe the more thankful I am that I live in America. I think we live in the best country. Maybe we haven't got all what we want to have but the poor people over here have got so much less. And they have to work like dogs to make a meager living. One good thing is that when I get back to where I belong I'll be satisfied to stay home and I won't have any desire for traveling.... it's so long since I got a letter from home that I'm almost stuck when it comes to writing one. And aside from being madder than a wet hen at these restrictions I can't say that I'm suffering in any way.

Osterholtz-Scharmbeck
February 20, 1946

Raymond didn't go to Bremen with his unit as he anticipated. Instead, he thought he had hit the jackpot when he was transferred out of the infantry and put on kitchen personnel. He called it the softest job in the army—the gravy train. He and a couple of other guys ran a huge mess hall with 50 Germans working under them. All Raymond had to do was stand around and look wise while the Germans did all the work. And their accommodations were what one would expect from a "white collar job": private showers, steam heat, a cleaning lady and the *the best chow I've had in the army.*

Osterholz-Scharmbeck was a town of 15,000 people, located in the heart of Germany's best farming country, 22 miles from Bremen. *And the best part is not one bomb fell on this town during the war so it's the most prosperous- looking town I've seen in Germany. But the people are still the same as all the rest of the Germans. They'd give their right arm for a pack of butts. I went to the barbershop for a haircut yesterday. The price of the haircut was one mark. I tried to pay the barber in money but he insisted he wanted two cigarettes instead. That's the cheapest haircut I've ever had and also one of the best!*

Has Ed come back from Minneapolis yet? I got a letter from him when I was in Marburg and it didn't sound like he was too crazy about city life. I don't blame him for that either. The best life is the farm where a guy can be free and do as he pleases. After I get back I'm not going to leave Roseau County for many years to come. I've seen enough people and enough of the world to last me for a long time. It's funny, no matter where you go there really is nothing that can compare with the place you come from. I guess it's like they say, a guy can be far away and still his heart is back home. I remember Ernie feeling this way. I only hope these months go fast so I can get back and start doing something useful again. I'm feeling pretty useless here right now.

February 26, 1946
Dear Mother, Dad and Brothers

I'm bored to death by this life of leisure. I can't stand to lay around day after day and do nothing. Today we had a few lessons on operating a field range. It turned out to be a pretty complicated gas stove so maybe we will have something to occupy our time for a few days anyway. We're supposed to be here learning to be cooks but these mess sergeants haven't got the ambition to teach us and we can hardly learn from the German cooks so I guess I'm doomed to this life of ease for a long time. I always thought when I was a civilian that I could live a soft life if it was offered to me, but I guess when a guy is used to working, that's the only way he can be happy.

Have you seen in the papers all the trouble they're having in the British zone of occupation? I guess the Germans are facing starvation there so they're starting to rebel. I don't blame them. The British have a way of making a mess out of things. A lot of Germans are also trying to get into the American zone from the Russian zone. A buddy of mine who speaks German talked with a young German girl who had just come back from near Berlin and the way she said she had some rough treatment at the hands of the Poles and Russians. I have yet to see an American soldier mistreat any Germans and I think we're the only army the Germans think are okay. I think that decent treatment will go a lot farther than kicking them around. Of course, the Americans are strict in their way too. Yesterday the intelligence guys in our outfit raided two houses in this town. They were under suspicion of running a black market and I guess they found plenty of stuff too. My buddy who speaks German went along as interpreter and he said that when they swooped down on the houses the occupants almost died from fright. Maybe next time they'll know enough to lay off the black market.

Spring is supposed to arrive here around the middle of April so it's a lot like Minnesota in that respect. I hope it comes soon. This is all I can get together today, and I know it's pretty dry reading. But I'm having a heck of a time writing letters when I don't get any from you.

Love,
Fat

Backnang
March 17, 1946

After Osterholz-Scharmbeck, Raymond's unit moved to Backnang in southern Germany. It was a country full of thin, hungry children who followed the soldiers around. Their faces were old and stringy-looking and their bellies were bloated from long hunger. Their big eyes had hardly any face around them—just big, hungry eyes. The soldiers almost went crazy trying to feed all of the children, but they soon found out that they could not do anything permanent and they felt ashamed, angry and helpless.

The people here in Backnan are pretty darn hungry. When the garbage is thrown out in back of the mess hall there's a whole bunch of women, kids, and men and they fight like cats and dogs for a few scraps of food. It makes me sick to even look at it. I can't see how we're going to build a better world without saving the people from starvation. But I guess this is the price Germany has to pay for trying to be the master race. They don't act like the master race now. When they meet a soldier on the sidewalk, most of them take to the streets. For my part I can't hate these people but I suppose it's because I haven't seen any action.

Raymond's assignment was to set up a mess hall, and the only option was to take over a dirty beer hall, which he did by hiring Germans and Poles to clean up the mess. It didn't take long before they had a smooth running mess hall. After the clean-up was complete, he said that all he had to do was walk around and look authoritative.

While in training, Raymond and the other soldiers were fed what they thought was propaganda about concentration camps and the killing of the Jews. Now they were receiving confirmation of these atrocities from the Germans themselves. *More than one German has admitted to me the horrible things they did to the Jews and they still hate them. But the Jews that are left are pretty well-protected.*

In a letter Raymond wrote to his brother Ed while he was stationed in Backnang, he talked more about the hunger he was witnessing in postwar Germany. *This morning we had to get an armed guard to chase the women away from the mess hall. They almost tore the GIs apart when they came out with their mess kits to go to the garbage cans. It's terrible to see people go hungry day after day. And the girls seem to be losing their morals. I haven't seen one yet that couldn't be bought for a few cigarettes or a little food. The better looking the daughter is the more the old lady makes the soldier pay for the honor of going to bed with her. And those of us who work in the kitchen get propositioned more often than anyone else. I've said it before but I'll say it again, Germany is paying a bitter price for the idea that she could dominate the world. I only want to get out of this hell hole and get back to where I don't have to see human misery everywhere and every day. I'm too soft-hearted to see people suffer and I feel so helpless. There's just not much we can do about the suffering other than help individual people, especially the children, whenever we can.*

Ed had just returned to the farm from a short sojourn in Minneapolis where he had gone to experience city life. Raymond writes: *So you've quit the city life and gone back on the farm again. Well, I can't say that I blame you. It's like you said that place where we live isn't the best place in the world but once you have lived there, it seems like it gets in your blood and you don't want to live any place else. I know that I haven't seen a place in all my travels that compares with Falun Township.*

It was only a few months ago that Raymond was complaining about the rigor of training, even wondering at times if he would be able to finish. Now he was unfavorably impressed with his relatively soft life, consisting of kitchen duty that required his attention but very little work. He didn't have to pull guard duty, as did the other guys in his unit, even though he was issued a helmet and a M1. He was convinced that the Germans were pretty well beaten down with no fight left in them.

Heilbronn

After two weeks in Backnang, his unit was sent to Heilbronn for a few days. Heilbronn was a town 30 miles away that the Americans had taken and lost three times during the fighting. It was in pretty bad shape, having been blown to pieces by bombs and artillery. The Allied air raids began in 1940, hitting the town about 20 times. Then in September, 1944, an air raid dropped 1100 bombs in one day, killing 280 residents. The catastrophic air raid for Heilbronn, though, was the bombing raid on December 4, 1944, when the city center was completely destroyed and the surrounding burroughs heavily damaged. Within one half hour 6500 people died, most incinerated beyond recognition.

The soft life that Raymond led in Backnang was replaced by hard work, necessitated by the formidable task of reconstruction. He was personally responsible for feeding 500 men three times a day in a huge mess hall. There was no Red Cross Club for entertainment during free time, so life was pretty tiresome. His mother had warned him about the black market and Raymond assured her that he would (mostly) stay away from any activity of that sort. Even so, he had a few cartons of cigarettes stolen while he was working by a civilian who sold them on the black market and then had the bad manners to tell Raymond all about it.

I keep thinking about Ernie, especially in times when I don't have anything to do. Ock and Ed were so much older than him and Roy was just a little guy, so Ernie and I were together most of the time. He respected his other brothers but he and I were like best friends. Maybe it's just being in the army that makes me think about him. I keep wondering what he would he would be like if he had lived. I think that he would have given the army some thought because he loved to fight and wasn't scared of anything or anyone. He loved hunting and the woods most of all, a lot like you, Mom.

I can't wait to get home and work with you guys in the woods. It sure will be nice to get a piece of timber and dig into the work I like.

Ludwigsburg
April 26, 1946

During World War II, the city of Ludwigsburg suffered moderate damage compared to other German cities. It was the site of a prisoner-of-war camp (Stalag V-A) from 1937 until 1945. Built in the 11th century, it had been used as a prison for hundreds of years. Raymond said that there were dungeons where they used to keep prisoners on black bread and water for as long as six months at a time.

After the war, Ludwigsburg served as a huge Displaced Persons camp for several thousand mostly Polish displaced persons until about 1948. There was also an Allied internment camp for war criminals in Ludwigsburg during 1945-1946. Raymond was stationed there for about a month in 1946. *Of course, Uncle Sam doesn't use dungeons here at this prison camp. In fact, the prisoners are pretty well-treated. We have quite a time keeping the Polacks who work in the kitchen from bumping off a German prisoner once in a while though. I've never seen two races of people carry such hatred for each other. Tonight about 7 o'clock I left the kitchen for about a half hour to start writing. I thought for sure the Polacks could wash the dishes and clean up the kitchen without me being there to watch them. But I was mistaken. When I came back to the kitchen about 7:30 they had rounded up a poor German prisoner and had him doing all the work while they sat around bossing him and calling him a Nazi. The prisoner was scared for his life. I returned him to his cell and put those Polacks back to work in a hurry. I think we're going to get German civilians to work in the kitchen. They seem to be more dependable.*

One of the German civilian workers at the camp asked Raymond if he could borrow the kitchen truck to pick up his monthly ration of wood. Raymond went with him to the wood yard where the guy who sold the wood put a few blocks in a big sack and weighed it to make sure that it didn't weigh more than 200 pounds. Raymond was both amused and saddened by that event. *Just think, 200 pounds of wood for one month! I thought to myself that you, Pa, can burn that in one night. And this poor guy has to provide heat and cooking fuel for his family for a whole month on this supply. I felt bad for him. But I see things over here that I wouldn't tell you about because it would make you cry, especially you, Mom.*

One of Raymond's assignments was to haul kitchen equipment and set up a kitchen for thirty American guards at one of the many concentration camps where the U.S. kept some of Germany's toughest Nazi war criminals. The dreary camp was built on a hill and surrounded by a high stone wall topped with barb wire entanglements and guarded by *trigger happy Polish guards who are ordered to shoot any German prisoner who comes within 15 feet of the wall.*

Today was a big day here at this prison camp. Fritz Kuhn walked to his freedom at 3 o'clock this afternoon. There were many high-brass and newspaper men here to see the steel gates close behind him. I'll bet they took his picture twenty times. He looked pretty happy about getting out and I can't say that I blame him.

Raymond talks about Fritz Kuhn as if his identity were well-known. Fritz Julius Kuhn was a Nazi anti-Semite who was the controversial head of the German-American Bund and arrested for misappropriation of Bund funds. He was arrested as an enemy agent after his release from prison and held by the federal government at an internment camp in Crystal City, Texas. His U.S. citizenship was cancelled on June 1, 1943. In 1945, he was released, sent to Ellis Island, and deported to Germany where he was imprisoned and released. He died in 1951 a poor and obscure chemist "unheralded and unsung."[26]

Raymond found that hanging around the kitchen day after day doing nothing but keeping the cooks on the ball was tiresome, and his thoughts turned toward home and things in his surroundings that reminded him of home. *Over here the farmers are going full blast in the fields just as you are, I'm sure. The Germans don't have much in the way of machinery. All you see are oxen and even milk cows pulling the plows. One day I saw a farmer seeding. He had a drill about four feet wide and a horse and a cow with a huge bag pulling it. It seems to me that the women do most of the work over here. They work in the fields all day and at night they go home with a big load of wood on their backs. The women in the States have it pretty soft compared to those over here. Not you though, Mom and Dad. One thing we guys can never say is that you have any easy days in your lives. I know for a fact that you are, as usual, busy planting a huge garden and doing hundreds of other jobs that have to be done on a farm.*

Think of what a happy day it will be when I can come home and we all can be together again. It isn't much more than seven months left now. I'm glad that I enlisted in the R.A. I don't believe all those rumors about fathers being sent home by September. I think that by the time Congress gets that bill through, I'll have been a civilian a long time. And we all know how those fat potbellies in Washington behave. Yesterday I got letters from Jean and Joan. I really get a kick out of hearing from those kids.

Asperg

Raymond wrote his second Mother's Day letter while he was holed up in Hohenasperg, an ancient fortress and prison overlooking Asperg. He had been in Asperg for a short time when he heard about thirty prisoners in solitary confinement who were going to be hanged. They were convicted of murdering American airmen so Raymond felt that they deserved their fate. He talked with one of the prisoners who had been on the Russian front and said that all the stories about the Nazis in Russia were true. *This guy said that they used to fill a house full of men, women and kids, lock the doors and set fire to it and then machine gun the ones who tried to escape through the windows. This guy's last wish before he died was to meet Hitler and repay him some of the hell he caused for the Germans. I saw him right before he went to the gallows. Pretty rough!*

May 12, 1946
Dear Mom,

Today is Mother's Day so I'm going to try and write a few lines to you. I planned on trying to get you a card in the PX but by the time my turn came they were all gone. But at least a letter is better than nothing. It shows that I remember you, Mom, and think of you a lot. I hope that you don't spend too much time worrying about me. You know that I can take care of myself and I manage to keep out of trouble pretty well. Over here the main thing is to mind your own business and there is no excuse for getting in trouble. At lot of the guys over here carry pistols and go around looking for trouble and they usually find it too. But for my part I never carry one and no one ever bothers me.

*We just got through with dinner and if I must say so myself, I made a dandy meal today. It was roast turkey, brown gravy, cranberry sauce, mashed spuds, peas, pastry, ice cream, bread and butter, and coffee. The guys were pretty satisfied. But tonight we're having stew for supper so I suppose I'll hear plenty of kick. Stew is something a soldier hates but we cannot eat good at every meal. I've only got so much ration for each week and that has to last. By the time I get home I should be a first class cook, Mom. Tomorrow I'm going up and see our BTRY (*Battery*) Commander and ask if I can't go to the Cooks and Bakers School in Frankfurt. It's a six-week course. He promised all of us new guys we could go when we first took control of the kitchen. Now it looks as if he must have changed his mind, but I'm going to still try. When I get home, I'll be able to help you in the* *kitchen a little. I remember Ernie use to tell me to help you out when he was sick. I didn't do much then except some chores. But when I get home I'll make it up to you and put my cooking skills to work.*

Boy, is it ever quiet around here today. Most of the guys have gone to Ludwigsburg on pass. I've never seen a place that can get so quiet as these prison walls. I sure wish you could see this place, Mom. When you get outside the prison walls and stand up on the hill you see some of the most beautiful scenery in the world. A person can forget that a war was ever fought in this part of the world. This place is hundreds of years old and all around the sides of the hill there are thick forests of spruce. Believe me, Mom, I spend a lot of my spare time walking those beautiful trails. You know how much I love the woods. I guess I got that from you. So did Ernie. Do you remember how he was the happiest when he was hunting? We shot a lot of rabbits together. Ock and Ed were the best deer hunters and Ernie really respected that. But I was the closest to him, mostly because we were close in age, I guess. I wish he had lived, Mom. I still miss him. I know that you do too.

I sure enjoy your letters, Mom, and can read every word in Norwegian. So don't stop writing. Tell Dad to write sometimes too. There's nothing that means more to a guy than to get a letter from your Dad and Mother. I can sit down and read a letter in Swedish or Norwegian just as easy as I can in English, so you never have to feel embarrassed about writing. Tell my brothers that I appreciate all the work they're doing on my land and that someday I hope to make it up to them. It's a nice thing to know when you're in the army that your land is being taken care of and not allowed to grow into weeds.

Love from your son,
Raymond

May 22, 1946

Raymond was bored. He heard about plans to raid some Germans suspected of dealing in the black market. Normally, a cook doesn't go on raiding parties, but he was so fed up with doing nothing that he asked the 1st sergeant if he could go along. Permission was granted, and Raymond was assigned the job of guarding the front door of the tavern where the raid was to occur. As soon as the GIs rushed in the Germans tried to get out, but they changed their minds when Raymond stuck his MI at them and clicked the safety off. Even though the GIs didn't find anything to arrest the Germans for, the excitement relieved some of the boredom in his life for a while. *These Black Marketers have an excellent grapevine and they probably knew about the raid before we pulled it. But we scared the daylights out of them, and it was fun while it lasted.*

In the same letter, Raymond asked his parents to send him a few cartons of cigarettes which, while inexpensive in the U.S., were like gold in Germany. He said that he sold two packs that morning for seven dollars but wasn't worried about the black market because as long as he entered the transaction in his currency control books there was no danger of getting pinched. He allowed as how he could send home at least a hundred bucks a month if his parents would send him the merchandise to sell.

Raymond was also homesick. He wrote letters every day to anyone who would write him back—letters to relatives in Norway and cousins in Chicago and Minneapolis as well to family and friends. He admitted to writing more letters in the 13 months he had been in the Army than he thought he was ever capable of writing. He loved getting letters from his daughter. *Jean was quick to write and tell me that she was the personal owner of one of the hogs that you recently purchased. That little squirt isn't bashful when it comes to asking for something. I guess she knows she can get whatever she asks for from Gappa and Gamma. Golly! I miss her an awful lot. I see the pictures I've received how big she's getting. It seems funny to think that only a little while ago she was a baby and it won't be too long before she's a young woman ready to make her own life. I sure hope that doesn't happen while I'm in the army!*

After several half-hearted attempts at receiving a promotion, he was promoted to Mess Sergeant, a job which he soon characterized as nerve-wracking. Gone was his soft life. Apparently, the GIs had some specific demands in the food department, one of which they had to be served at the same time for every meal. When that didn't happen, the Mess Sergeant suffered verbal abuse, so much so that Raymond found himself longing for the soft set up—the one he thought was boring—he had before the promotion.

There was also constant worry about the food shortage all over the world. Raymond had to keep track of every piece of food he allowed to be used in the mess hall. Sugar was the most rationed commodity. *Last week we drew fifty pounds of sugar for 56 men and out of that I'm supposed to get pastry baked and have sugar on the table besides. It doesn't take any expert to know that can't be done. It isn't my fault if I don't get the stuff. This job is one big headache.*

He ended a particularly frustrating letter on a positive note which had as its basis a deal he made with a D.P. (Displaced Person) Polish guard. He traded a carton of cigarettes for a "dandy" pair of German field glasses. He enjoyed climbing up in one of the guard towers on the hill to see *small villages just as plain as if I was right on top of them and I could hardly see them with the naked eye. These glasses are going to be handy to have at home.*

June 20, 1946
Dear Mother, Dad, and Brothers,

Well, I'm still the top kick here in the mess hall but if the Colonel at BN (Battalion) *doesn't soon cough up a few stripes he'll have to get another Mess. Sgt. I'm not going to do a Staff Sgts. work as a Pfc so I'm going to plug along and run this joint for another two weeks. And then if I don't get a rating I'll go back to being 1*st *cook. At least I didn't have any worries on my mind then.*

Everything is pretty quiet in the old castle right now but not for long. Tonight the GIs are pretty excited about the Joe Louis fight and there's a lot of betting going on. We're getting up at 3:30 in the morning to listen to the fight. I think for my part that Louis will whip Conn again. Who are you guys picking to win?

The way the people live over here just doesn't compare with the way we got it back in the States. And I don't mean only now. I guess it's always been this way. Have I told you about the women, how they seem to be doing most of the work? Right now it's haying season and I've seen women go at least a mile from their house in the village and cut hay with a scythe and haul it home in a wheelbarrow for the cow or two that she's got. The more fortunate ones might have an ox to do the hauling. Man, it seems funny for an American to see this when we're used to modern machinery.

How are the crops coming along back home? Over here in Southern Germany they really are nice. It makes me homesick to see the waving fields of grain and to smell the fragrance of the freshly cut hay. It makes me long for my own little farm—to be back there and work in my own fields once more. I guess I was meant to be a farmer, not a soldier but I don't know many guys who are meant to be soldiers.

It's a good thing the people here are going to have a good crop because they need it so badly. There are an awful lot of hungry people in Germany. Many are getting real thin and run down looking. When I go out and buy potatoes from them I bring a little soap or maybe a pound of coffee or sugar. They smell the coffee first and then want to trade potatoes for the coffee. If they're real poor, I give them some coffee or sugar in exchange for just a few potatoes. Seeing all of these hungry people, especially, the kids, gives a guy a hopeless feeling because there's not much you can do to help.

This is all for now. But I'll write again soon.

Love from Fat

August 2, 1946

Until 1943, Hohenasperg was used as a way station for gypsy populations who were being sent to concentration camps. A book published in 1999 tells about a 13-year-old American boy who was deported to Germany after the war and treated like a war criminal by the United States government. When he arrived in Hohenasperg, he was put in a prison cell and forced to live like a Nazi. His fellow inmates were high-ranking officers of the Third Reich who were being held for interrogation and denazification. All attempts to convince the American guards that he was an American failed.[27]

Personnel at the castle were being cut every day, until there were only 25 men left. Most of the prisoners had been discharged and it didn't appear as if more would be brought in. For all intents and purposes, Camp 76 was finished as an internment. But Raymond hoped that it would exist until he was discharged. Every day, soldiers left for the States, and Raymond was counting the days until he would be going up the gangplank, heading for the place where he really wanted to be.

He was still doing a Staff Sergeant's work as a Pfc. No stripes had been given to anyone at Asperg. The word from the Camp Commander was that the ratings were frozen, so no stripes could be awarded. Raymond was past the point of caring about stripes. In fact, he seemed to derive some satisfaction from giving orders. One day he ordered three prisoners to paint the kitchen: one was a banker who still owned a large bank in New York and the other two were lawyers. *It's funny to think that these guys who once made people jump when they talked now are glad to wield a paint brush in order to get a square meal. It's a fickle world, isn't it?*

The Germans' hatred for the Jews surfaced in Raymond's letters with one story after another. One such story took place on a hot summer night when a riot broke out between the two races of people. Armed soldiers in Camp 76 were called out to put down the riot, which they did but not easily. Raymond had lost a lot of the respect he once had for the German soldiers, especially when they kept insisting that the German army was the best in the world and laughed at the American soldiers who disputed that fact. *For my part, if anyone laughed at me I would make him wish he hadn't. What I wish is that we could all get along, even the Germans and the Jews. The war is over. Why can't we make the hard part of putting the country together again a little easier?*

While Raymond lacked respect for the German soldier, he had nothing but admiration for the German people and their work ethics. *The Krauts are getting ready for a rough winter, with little food and clothing. They work night and day to harvest a darn nice crop and when I say work I mean it. I've only seen one binder and that was an American made McCormick Deering. The rest of them are going at it with scythes, working so hard on a little black bread and potatoes. Even the kids who are Jean and Joan's age are out in the field helping tie the grain into bundles.*

As the time for his discharge drew nearer, Raymond grew more homesick and nostalgic. And he worried—about things such as whether he was becoming lazy and so soft that he wouldn't be able to do a hard day's work when he arrived back home. He was cutting meat one day when his right hand blistered in three places from just pressing on the knife. He took that as a sign that he would never be able to work a bow saw as a lumberjack again. He worried that all the work on the farm would be done by the time he got home, so he wouldn't be able to do his share again. He wished he were working harder while he was in the Army so he wouldn't feel that he was wasting the best days of his life.

It turned out that Camp 76 wasn't finished as an internment, after all. One night the Company Commander gave the order to go to Ludwigsburg and pick up 500 German prisoners from South America. That kind of work was not a part of Raymond's job but they were short of drivers in the motor pool, so he was asked to take the kitchen truck and help out. He grabbed the chance to alleviate his boredom and jumped in a two and one half ton truck that had lost its muffler... . *you ought to have heard the roar when I double clutched it down from 4th to 3rd. I suppose the MPs will make me put a muffler on but, until they do, I'm going to make myself heard which is not an easy thing to do around here.*

October 14, 1946
Dear Dad, Mom, and Brothers,

I never thought I'd still be here in Germany but I'm still waiting for orders to ship. If this shipping strike doesn't end I might be here some time yet. The P.O.E. at Bremerhaven is jammed with troops waiting shipment home. And the food supply for the GIs is getting pretty bad. If they don't settle that strike soon we'll be living on potatoes only. I bought my first hunting license in Germany the other day. The 1st sergeant and the motor sergeant and I went out to try our luck and saw plenty of rabbits but they were going too fast to hit. We were carrying carbines which hold 15 shots a piece. So you should have heard the barrage when we all turned loose on a rabbit. Tomorrow we're going up in some real deer country in the Black Forest. I wish I could be home and hunt this fall but I guess that's out of the question so I'll enjoy tomorrow.

It's been two weeks since I heard from Myrtle so I'm really starting to wonder what in the world is wrong. And it's so long since any of you at home has written that I think you've forgotten about me.

What do you think about all the talk of war with Russia? The rumors are going pretty hot over here and the Germans are spreading all the propaganda they can to help start it. If that war starts one big Russian drive could take the whole of Germany and France. We've only got one Division that's up to full fighting strength and we all know how prepared Russia is. Here's hoping it stays a rumor and never starts.

I was at the Company in Ludwigsburg this morning and the 1st sergeant said that the 60th infantry leaves on maneuvers the 23rd of this month. Boy, I sure hope they ship me home before that comes. Maneuvers this time of the year are pretty tough. The guys have to sleep in tents and eat outside so you can imagine the difficult situation. This camp is going to break up in a few days and be taken over by German civilians and Polish guards. So if I don't get out of here fast I'll wind up pulling guard on some lonely bivouac area.

How are Myrt and Jean getting along? I suppose they have moved out East by this time. I know there isn't much wood out there but I'm sure that you guys will keep the home fires burning until I get home. I got the picture that Myrt sent me of Roy and Margaret with Judy. She sure is a good-looking kid and Roy is a pretty proud-looking guy. Is that a new chicken coup I saw on a picture? Did you put a cement floor in it? It sure looks like a dandy. You were entitled to a new coop because the old one was getting pretty run down. You wrote and asked me one time, Ed, if I could pick up a few things for you over here, but you never did say what so let me know.

Some time ago Myrt wrote that Pop had been to the doctor for some treatments but she didn't say what for. I would like to know what the treatments were for. How are you feeling now, Mom? I suppose that you've got as much to do as ever. I've been thinking so much about that dandy potato soup you used to make. I remember that Ernie loved that soup too and kept saying in his letters that he couldn't wait to have some when he got home. I don't remember if he was well enough to have some when he got home though. Well, that's the first meal I'm going to have when I arrive. Don't forget that.

Well, this isn't much of a letter but it will have to do for now. Drop me a line when you find time and give my regards to Joseph if he's around. If I'm lucky any letter you write now will have to be sent to the States, but I'm probably going to be here in Germany for some time yet.

Love from Fat

Bremerhaven

Bremerhaven was a key base for the German navy from 1935-1945. Most of the city was destroyed by the World War Two bombings. Some parts of the port, however, were spared by the Allied forces because they needed the harbor for supplies after the War.

October 30, 1946
Dear Mom, Dad and Brothers

Just a few lines to let you know that I'm here in the P.O.E. I've been here 3 days now and I still haven't heard when we're supposed to be leaving. It could be 8 or 9 days. I can't see what they're holding us up for. I counted 8 big ships in the Harbor today so there shouldn't be any shortage of shipping. Boy, I can hardly wait until I set foot on U.S. soil again. I'm anxious to get home and make myself useful again. If I would have been in good shape now I could have been discharged as soon as I hit the States but it's no use to get out of the Army without making them put me back in shape.

So, pretty soon I'll be a veteran. I can't help but think that what I've done and my service isn't enough to deserve that title. The guys who saw battle and whose lives were in danger, they're the ones who deserve the title. I never saw battle and never felt that my life was in real danger. The closest I came to fear was in training when I thought I would be going over. But then the war ended. Thank God for that. I guess the only thing I can say is that I went where I was told to go and did what I was told to do. I've given 18 months to the military. I guess I can rightfully be called a veteran.

It sure is going to be nice to see you all again. It seems so long since I saw you all last I can hardly remember it. But it won't be long now. Don't worry about me.

Love Fat

Afterword

I've always been intrigued by the idea of discovering old letters hidden away in an attic. The idea became a reality a few summers ago when I discovered Ernie's letters while rooting around in the upstairs of my grandparents' house. I eagerly read the letters with a strong desire to know the writer and the time during which he lived. I never knew Ernie; in fact, my father didn't know him either since he was too young to remember much about his brother's life and death. Uncle Raymond did his best to satisfy my curiosity with stories about Ernie, but I was hungry to know more about this courageous teenage boy who became ill at a time when little was known about his illness and its treatment. I asked myself what he must have been thinking while dealing with his illness in a city, far away from his parents and the farm he loved. The disease itself was cruel enough, but to suffer without his family in unfamiliar surroundings had to have been the cruelest of all fates. I wondered about these things.

    The poignancy of the letters made me cry—not eyes-welling-up-with-tears- crying, but raw, unchecked bawling. The letters were too sad, too sweet, too innocent and too full of hopeless hope for me to read all at once. So I read a few at a time, sometimes going for days without reading any. But my desire to learn about this boy who didn't live long enough to be my uncle was so strong that I kept reading, all the time filling in the details of a sad story plot: boy becomes ill during the Great Depression; is forced to receive treatment far from home; dreams of returning to the farm he loved; remains hopeful until the end; but dies anyway. When I finished, I felt that I had a finished portrait of fifteen-year-old Ernie, along with a deep appreciation of his love for his parents and brothers and his home on the farm.

Ernie's letters provided me with some insight into the character of Tom, a boy Ernie's age with no last name, who was in the hospital at the same time, battling a disease that also had no name. He was one of the 250,000 young people riding the rails from town to town trying to find work that would put food in their bellies, something their parents were unable to do during this tragic time. Tom was someone's son. Did anyone know the extent of his illness? Did he see his mother before he died? Was he alone after Ernie left the hospital? Those questions remained unanswered. While Tom's story is similar to Ernie's (except that they were forced to leave home for different reasons), his portrait that emerges from the letters is anything but complete. There is no closure to his story, but there is comfort in knowing that Tom was in the hospital with Ernie. They were there for each other.

I could have ended my story with Ernie and Tom. It would have been a natural ending. However, there was the matter of a second batch of letters I found, inviting me into another world that was both removed from and inextricably tied to Ernie's. Thirteen years after Ernie's death, Raymond, a soldier in World War II, wrote letters home that were sprinkled with memories of his brother. It occurred to me that joining these two lives in one book, without a solid transition, required a leap of faith on my part that the reader would be able to understand and appreciate the connection. Since I wanted to write about both uncles, I took that leap.

Fat returned home from the war to his 80 acres across the road from my dad and lived there until he died at 89. He farmed his land and worked as a lumberjack for many years. Growing up, I asked questions about his military experience but never learned much beyond the fact that he was a cook in the Army. While he was reluctant to talk about things that he saw, felt, or thought during his tour of duty, he willingly and easily wrote about them in letters that remained hidden for fifty years. Because of his letters, I was able to fill in the details of a part of Uncle Raymond's life of which I knew very little. A complete portrait emerged, just as it had done in the case of Ernie.

Ernie's and Raymond's letters were similar in obvious ways. The comparison breaks down with an examination of one important concept: hope. They both wrote consistently and longingly of their hope for a return to the farm and the people who lived there. Raymond's hope, however, was more realistic, especially when it was clear that he would not be going into battle. His hope was not "if" but "when." Ernie's hope, on the other hand, began with the "when" but increasingly became an "if," until it diminished to the point where the reader knew that if Ernie were to return to the place he loved, it would be to die. I think that, at the end, even Ernie accepted the hopelessness of believing otherwise.

This book is a tribute to honor the memories of three people, all of whom impacted my life in some way. I am grateful for the opportunity to learn about Ernie, who was courageously persistent in his determination not to worry his family about the severity of his illness and his homesickness. He introduced me to Tom who, along with being a real person, represented a segment of the population that symbolized courage and resilience during our country's Great Depression. I have the utmost respect and admiration for the memory of those young people who rode the rails, mostly out of desperation to survive during this time. As for my Uncle Raymond, I wish that I would have said "Thank you" while he was still alive. I would have added, "The fact that you didn't serve in a theater of war simply means that you were not called to do so. It does not mean that you weren't ready to go. The combat troops couldn't have done the job without soldiers like you who supported them in some way. Thank you for your service to our country."

Notes

1. In a Valedictory address Dr. Osler gave to the University of Pennsylvania on May 1, 1889.
2. See Patberg, et al, for a history of the Sven Pearson family.
3. On the evolution of Hodgkins lymphoma treatment, see Cavallo; for more information, consult the *lymphoma information* Website.
4. For information about children and Hodgkin lymphoma, consult *cancer.gov* Web site.
5. James San Jude from *What Life was Like During the Great Depression* by Uys.
6. See Klingaman, Minehan, Freedman, Uys, and Eganfor detailed descriptions of life during the Great Depression.
7. Minehan and Uys wrote about the boys and girls who rode the rails during the Great Depression.
8. In an interview with Don Snyder at his home in Toledo, Ohio.
9. From *A Hobo Memoir 1936* by Fawcett.
10. For a sympathetic view of Al Capone, read *Capone, the Other Image* by Michele.

11. Information on medicine and health in the 1930s.
12. For a detailed description of hobos in the 1930s, read the Fawcett memoir.
13. See Nathiel and Hill for a detailed chronicle of World War II.
14. Wouk's novel, *War and Remembrance*, personalizes the Battles of the Coral Sea, Midway, and Guadalcanal, along with other battles in the Pacific Theater.
15. See Nathiel and Hill.
16. Nathiel and Hill.
17. Tom Brokaw's trilogy—*The Greatest Generation, The Greatest Generation Speaks,* and *An Album of Memories*—provides information and personal histories regarding the sacrifice and courage of the men and women who lived and fought during the Depression and World War II.
18. Bradley's portrayal of Japanese fanaticism during the hard-fought Battle of Iwo Jima.
19. Nathiel and Hill.
20. *No Ordinary Time* by Doris Kearns Goodwin.
21. Goodwin.
22. See Goodwin for a discussion of Roosevelt's wartime leadership errors; also, consult the United States Holocaust Memorial Museum article on World War II in Europe.
23. *An Album of Memories* by Brokaw.
24. From the Web site on the post-war reconstruction in Germany.

25. The information on the various German cities—Marburg, Osterholtz- Scharmbeck, Backnang, Heilbron Ludwigsburg Asperg and Bremerhaven—was gathered from Wikipedia.
26. Fritz Kuhn at Google.com.
27. *The Prison called Hohenasperg: An American Boy Betrayed by his Government During World War 11* by Jacobs.

References

Alter, J. (2006). *The Defining Moment.* Simon and Schuster: New York.

Bradley, J. (2000). *Flags of our Fathers.* Bantam Books: New York.

Brokaw, T. (2004). *An Album of Memories*, Random House: New York.

Brokaw, T. (1998). *The Greatest Generation.* Random House: New York.

Brokaw, T. (1999). *The Greatest Generation Speaks.* Random House: New York.

Cavallo, J. (2008). The evolution of Hodgkin lymphoma treatment: A glance in the past and what's ahead. *Lymphoma Today,* Summer, Vol. 6 (2), p. 6.

Childhood Hodgkin Lymphoma Treatment. National Cancer Institute. www.cancer.gov//childhodgkins/. http://www.lymphomainfo.net/lymphoma/comparison.html.

Egan, T. (2006). *The Worst Hard Time.* Houghton Mifflin: New York.

Fawcett, J. (1994). A hobo memoir 1936. *Indiana Magazine of History, XC*, December.

Freedman, R. (2005). *Children of the Great Depression*. Clarion Books: New York.

Goodwin, D.K. (1994). *No Ordinary Time*. Simon and Schuster: New York.

Hill, D. (Ed.) (2004). *Chronicles of War*. Transatlantic Press: Hartfordshire, UK.

Jacobs, A.D. (1999). *The Prison Called Hohenasperg: An American Boy Betrayed by his Government During World War II*. Universal Publishers: New York.

Klingaman, W.K. (1989). *1929: The Year of the Great Crash*. Harper and Row: New York.

Michele, A.J, (1978). Capone, the other image. *Good Old Days*. February, p. 40.

Minehan, T. (2009). *Boy and Girl Tramps of America*. http://xroads.virginia.edu/-MAOI/white/anthology/tramps.htm/.

Nathiel, R. (1985). *Atlas of World War II*. Brompton Books Corp: New York.

Osler, W. (1910). *Aequanimities and other Addresses* (2nd Ed.). Blakiston's Son and Co.: Philadelphia.

Patberg, J.P. and Pearson, M.C. (2005). *We Just Shoveled Two Feet of Partly Cloudy: A (Mostly) Minnesota Memoir*. Soleil Press: Lisbon Falls, Maine.

Snyder, Donald (Personal Communication).

The 1930s: Medicine and Health: Overview. www.encyclopedia.com.

United States Holocaust Memorial Museum. *Holocaust Encyclopedia*. http://www.ushmm.org/w/c/en/ModuleId=10005143.

Uys, E.L. (2003). *Riding the Rails: Teenagers on the Move During the Great Depression.* TV Books: New York.

Uys, E.L. (2009). *What Life was Like During the Great Depression.* http://erroluys.com.

Wouk, H. (1978). *War and Remembrance.* Pocket Books: New York.

www.ingramcontent.com/pod-product-compliance
Lightning Source LLC
LaVergne TN
LVHW021712060526
838200LV00050B/2632